Department of English Local Hi
OCCASIONAL PAPERS
Fourth Series   Edited by Charle
Number 1

Re-thir   English Local History

CHARLES PHYTHIAN-ADAMS, M.A., F.S.A., F.R.Hist.S.
Head of the Department of English Local History,
University of Leicester

 LEICESTER UNIVERSITY PRESS 1987

First published in 1987 by Leicester University Press

Designed by Douglas Martin
Filmset in Linotron 202 Palatino
by Alan Sutton Ltd, Gloucester
Printed in Great Britain by Antony Rowe Ltd, Chippenham

Cover: A lesser market centre within a *pays*: 'Stow in the Wold, Gloucestershire' in the
mid-nineteenth century (unidentified engraver).

British Library Cataloguing in Publication Data

Phythian-Adams, Charles
Re-thinking English local history. – (Occasional papers/Department of English
Local History, Leicester University. Fourth series: no. 1)
1. Great Britain – History, Local
I. Title II. Series
942 DA1

ISBN 0-7185-2041-6

Contents

List of maps

Acknowledgments

The initial impetus to write this paper came from two friends of English local history: Mr Peter Boulton, the ever-helpful Secretary of the Leicester University Press, who first suggested it; and Professor Peter Clark – now Director of the Urban History Centre at Leicester University – who gave me the chance to give a preliminary airing to some of the ideas contained herein (under the title 'Little Images of the Great Country'), at the stimulating conference which he and others organized at Williamsburg, Virginia, in September 1985, on the subject of 'The Social World of Britain and America, 1600–1820'. Beyond them it would be invidious to single out from many those who have been either influential over numerous years or helpfully critical in this present connection, but I cannot forbear to mention Anne Barker, Jill Bourn, Mary Carter, Alan Everitt, Gary Lewitt, Evelyn Lord, Richard McKinley, Anne Mitson, Alan Storm, Margery Tranter, Sue Wright, and, most particularly, Keith Snell, David Hey and Harold Fox who have read and constructively criticized either this text or its predecessor. I am also especially grateful to Mr Peter Gray of Bedford College of Higher Education who has liberally laid at my disposal his own work on the 1841 census for Bedfordshire – an outcome, it should be said, of his personal contribution to a seminar on the present subject which I gave at that excellent College in 1985. Neither he, nor anyone else, however, can be held responsible for the views expressed below.

Intellectual debts are one thing; practical help is another. On this occcasion I am grateful yet again to those who have rallied at short notice with regard to the creation and re-creation of a typescript: to Dorothy Brydges and most especially to Muriel Phillips. To Iris Browning and Judy Nicol my fervent thanks are also due in other respects too numerous to list. Susan Martin of the Leicester University Press has been exceptionally helpful over the finalization of the text.

Charles Phythian-Adams, University of Leicester

Foreword

> In some quarters, its reputation is low because academics still need to be convinced that local history will not direct students into parochial studies, irrelevant to the broad historical movements which are considered by them to be an undergraduate's proper concerns.
>
> (*Report of the Committee to Review Local History*, under the chairmanship of Lord Blake, 1979, para. 8.04)

Thanks to the support of the Leicester University Press, it is now nearly 35 years of continuous publication since this series of Occasional Papers was launched by H.P.R. Finberg with what was, in effect, a manifesto for the academic study of local history. Since the delivery of *The Local Historian and his Theme*, as an introductory lecture in 1952,[1] however, the scope and nature of the subject has expanded to such an extent that the start of a fourth series of Occasional Papers seems an appropriate moment at which to mark and review these developments, and to do so in the longer-term context of the sometimes uneasy relationship between 'national' history and 'local' history. There is still a good deal of misunderstanding about the aims of academic local history today, as there is about the forms of explanation which some of its practitioners have been and still are evolving. So extraordinarily fertile in ideas has this period been, moreover, that it also seems timely to pause and take stock of the subject from within.

The content of English local history is constantly being re-thought, but perhaps as befits the nature of the subject, the process of re-thinking tends to be pragmatic. Very little attention is paid to the conceptual aspects of its concerns despite the fact that these are worthy of critical scrutiny. It may well be indeed that both in practice *and* in theory, academic local historians should be redefining the priorities which they accord to the objects of their study not only at the 'community' level but also at a wider variety of socio-spatial levels, where the local and the national more conspicuously interact, than is currently the case in much contemporary local historical writing. No more than 'national' history can 'local' history afford to be introverted in its aims; no definition of the local historical quest, therefore, can ignore the nature of the relationship between local and national history.

This essay then will be concerned above all with the ways in which academic local historians have ever looked more widely than their immediate concerns might imply, and how in the future it might prove possible for them to connect more systematically still with the history of English society as a whole. To aspire to such an aim, it will be necessary to pay particular attention at first to the manner in which local historians have themselves defined the wider significances of their studies, and following from this, to scrutinize critically the units of investigation that they have adopted to these ends. Since, moreover, the concerns of local historians have both shifted and widened over the last 35 years, it will not be before time to ask uncomfortable questions: can the subject now boast a wider frame of reference; and if it can, to what extent are those established units of investigation still relevant? To seek answers to such questions, and to seek them in the light of a national context, is also to look, however briefly, beyond the remit of local history towards those historical approaches most relevant to its central preoccupations as they are currently practised at a national level. Without that perspective, and indeed without some understanding of the short-comings of that practice, it would be impossible to assess the extent to which the conventional objects of local historical analysis are any longer appropriate.

From these viewpoints, it will be argued that because of the extensive but inevitably piecemeal achievements of local historians over the last generation, the time has indeed now come to think radically about the central aims of the subject, and in the light of those aims, to create some sort of conceptual framework within which both old and new units of investigation may be fitted. An attempt will then be made, in a highly generalized way, to build on certain existing trends, both within the subject itself and in cognate fields of research, towards such a possible new framework, in order to furnish a fresh vantage point from which to review some of the structures inherent in the provincial societies of England's past. This essay seeks, therefore, to open up for debate a wider definition of the scope of English local history as an academic subject, and to proffer tentatively an alternative way in which local historians might relate their miniature compositions to the broader canvas of national history.

The express purpose of this paper, then, is to link back with Finberg's definition of the subject in the particular context of the Leicester approach (or, more correctly, approaches) which he and W. G. Hoskins created: an approach which has always sought to view the subject comparatively across the country as a whole, and which has been continuously evolved in the Department of English Local History ever since its foundation in 1948 at the then University College of Leicester. Not only does this mean that the emphasis here will be on approaches to the 1500-year history of the ever-changing 'pre-industrialized tradition', simply because that has been until recently the speciality of the department; it means also that the view of the subject's development will largely be a 'Leicester' one if that is generously defined. When Asa Briggs coined the phrase 'The Leicester School of local historians', he went on to say, 'scattered though they are'.[2] By this he meant to include all the contributor to the books he was then reviewing: not only those who were then, or had formerly been, connected with the Leicester department, but also those elsewhere who were in sympathy with its concerns. That too will be the criterion adopted here, though without in any way intending that the reputations of such independent scholars should be seen as somehow enhancing the standing of Leicester, or denying that they have individual historical approaches of their own. Conversely, in an essay of this length, some self-imposed statute of limitations has had to be set. This should not be read as an exhaustive bibliographical comment on the entire development of the field: only contributions to the framework, as opposed to the detail, of the subject will here receive attention.

Chapter 1

Local History and National History

The business of the local historian, then, as I see it is to re-enact in his own mind, and to portray for his readers, the Origins, Growth, Decline, and Fall of a local community.

(H. P. R. Finberg, *The Local Historian and His Theme*, 1952, p.9)

At the heart of the modern practice and justification of academic local historical writing there lies a tacit creative tension – an apparent contradiction even – in the way in which the subject is perceived as relating to the history of national developments: that is, in the terminology of H. P. R. Finberg, the tension between 'national history localized' and 'local history *per se*'.

The practice of 'national history localized' – the exploration of 'national' themes at local levels – may boast a long and distinguished academic pedigree, and it has been reflected in the writings of many of our most eminent national historians – historians so diverse as F. M. Stenton, Eleanora Carus-Wilson, Joel Hurstfield and J. H. Plumb – and not least within the general regional discussions to be found amongst the magisterial pages of the *Victoria History of the Counties of England*. In terms of the development of English local history as an academic discipline in its own right, moreover, it is relevant to note that three of the pioneers of the subject as it later came to be practised, emerged out of this tradition. For G. H. Tupling who, in his analysis of the economic history of Rossendale, placed great emphasis on the developments of the sixteenth and seventeenth centuries, that period offered 'perhaps more valuable contributions than any other, by way of illustration and contrast, to the record of national development'.[1] In the case of J. D. Chambers, his study of eighteenth-century Nottinghamshire sought 'to show the movement of local history during the period preceding the Industrial Revolution on the background of national history, and local material that cannot be related to the facts of national history either as an example of, or as an addition to, existing knowledge has been generally excluded.' Again, he stressed, this work 'is essentially an attempt to use local history in the service of general history and it is addressed to those students and teachers who regard local history in the light of a means, not an end.'[2] For W. G. Hoskins, his study of Exeter between 1688 and 1800 was primarily, though far from wholly, a contribution to the history of the serge industry during that period. Not only did his book arise out of an M.A. thesis on the industry in the West country generally, the leading area of production in the country, but Exeter was taken to express the essence of the subject. Exeter more or less monopolized the whole outport trade in serges and in the context of their production Hoskins could state: 'The industrial history of Exeter during this period is almost entirely the history of the serge industry.'[3]

More than this, it is instructive to note that in the very same year as Finberg first defined the thematic concern of the 'Leicester School' as 'local history *per se*', both he and Hoskins are to be found introducing the collection of essays, which they published under the title *Devonshire Studies*, in the following terms:

> Some of the following studies deal with aspects of the Devonshire past which have appealed to us as interesting in themselves. Others are concerned not so much with local history *per se* as with English history localized in Devon. The mixture of force and forbearance by which the kings of Wessex pushed their frontier westward; the part which personal intrigue has played in shaping the county boundaries; the colonization and settlement of the countryside; the vicissitudes of families; the growth and decay of towns; the fortunes of the yeomanry and gentry; the lot of the farm labourer: these are themes of more than parochial import.

Again

> For the best part of a thousand years Tavistock has combined, on a small scale indeed, but in a state of high perfection, the most characteristic elements of English feudal, monastic, parliamentary and industrial history. Few other towns are so historically representative.[4]

The thematic dependence of local history on national history reappears as a constant thread in Finberg's various theoretical expositions of the former subject. If 'Barchester stands out as a distinct articulation, not only of the national community, but of Western society as a whole', nevertheless 'it remains true that a study of the whole will do more to enlighten us about any single part than vice versa.'[5] Thus, 'to treat it [local history] as an introduction or a contribution to national history, is to invert the true relationship between them.' Local historians, Finberg insisted, must come to their subject 'well grounded in the history of England'.[6] In 1962, he asserted: 'We may picture the family, the local community, the national state and the supra-national society as a series of concentric circles. Each requires to be studied with constant reference to the one outside it; . . .'[7]

If an element of 'national history localized' thus survived in Finberg's thinking, the quotation just given nevertheless ended with the words '. . . but the inner rings are not the less perfect for being wholly surrounded and enclosed by the outer.' For at one and the same time, Finberg was claiming that local history was to be seen 'not as an ancillary discipline but as one subsisting in its own right. Those who take up this position – and without more ado let me avow that I am one of them – draw a distinction between local history *per se* and national history localized.'[8] The objects of local historical inquiry could thus be studied in their own rights and for their own sakes. The local societies in question did have distinctive histories deserving of individual attention; they had existed at wholly different spatial levels from the society of the nation; and their origins, their varying chronological developments and, where relevant, their physical extinctions (or even the spiritual extinction of their traditional cultures) were to be measured on time-scales quite different to that more generally experienced by the nation as an historically conceived whole. Instead of merely illustrating known national trends, therefore, the local historian, Finberg implied, should study local societies – or 'communities' as he called them – for what they were: localized and highly variable expressions not simply of powerful historial trends, but as singular expressions of the wider contemporaneous society in which they were implanted. To that same end, both he and Hoskins separately defined a thematic programme of basic socio-economic questions that went far beyond pre-existing approaches to the study of localities; questions that related to such fundamental human concerns as settlement, personal or communal survival, and settlement desertion. It was an approach that thus concentrated on such matters as securing a foothold on the land, getting a living, adaptation to institutional or technical innovation (successfully or otherwise), and so on. Above all, it was insisted, no past local community could be properly understood without some knowledge also of the particular environment in which it was situated. In other words, the essential precondition of a localized study was a close attention to topographical variation.[9]

In Hoskins's later thinking, indeed, these ideas about local societies and landscapes were taken even further and towards more abstract levels still. By 1965, his general interests were shifting increasingly towards the study of population and epidemics on the one hand, and to grain-supplies and harvest crises on the other. Accordingly, he stated, 'I believe . . . that local history properly conceived and practised by professionally trained workers is, . . . a science of Human Ecology.' By this he meant:

> We should be studying living human communities and their reaction to their
> environment, and to change in that environment over the past 2,000 years. Among
> animals and plants a high mortality in Nature serves to maintain a working balance
> of population and food supply. How did the human race adapt itself to the
> limitations of its local environment? Can one define an *ecosystem* for human beings at
> some historical period? What are the criteria?[10]

Finberg's and Hoskins's insistence on what Professor Maurice Beresford has happily dubbed 'the biography of Little Places'[11] as a pursuit quite distinct from that of national history, reflected a novel departure from the then academic historical conventions. Finberg's opening paper in the first series of these Occasional Papers, indeed, represented no less than a resounding theoretical declaration of unilateral independence for a wholly fresh historical approach.

Seminal as the writings of Hoskins and Finberg both have been, however, their few and briefly generalized theoretical statements were but barely matched by their own practices of the subject. Where both have been most influential on scholarly thinking, indeed, has been not solely in the field of local revelation – local history *per se* – but at that level where, as M. M. Postan once warmly acknowledged, '"Local" studies appear to be conceived as contributions towards a generalized view of English developments.'[12] In other words, the originality of both scholars lay not in the localization of established 'national' themes but in what might be described *per contra* as the 'nationalization' of freshly conceived localized themes. On this view, academic local studies did not merely sophisticate or mildly question established 'text book' generalization. Such studies suggestively threw up potentially new 'national' themes for wider consideration. To press the point, it is only necessary here to recall the two major areas of investigation in which each of these scholars was most deeply concerned. Finberg's fundamental challenge to the then established view on the discontinuity between Roman and Anglo-Saxon England in his *Roman and Saxon Withington* (1956) ended assertively *à propos* the possibilities of the early estate records of the Worcester diocese which he had sampled for his own analysis: 'A detailed study of the group as a whole, using the modern techniques of local history, would certainly uncover many secrets, and might resolve some at least of those perplexities with which the beginnings of English society are still surrounded'.[13] As he himself had just demonstrated, if this was local history *per se*, it was also local history with a potentially national dimension. Equally transcendent of a localized theme was, as its title implied, Hoskins's classic work *The Midland Peasant*. As he himself stated categorically:

> This book . . . is a contribution to English economic and social history, and not a history of the village as such. With this in mind I have rejected a considerable amount of material that would ordinarily have gone into a local history as generally understood and which

– shades of Chambers 25 years earlier –

> would doubtless have interested the people of Wigston and its neighbourhood . . . This is a study of a peasant culture, of the way in which it was built up (so far as we can discover it), of the way it worked, and of the way in which it finally dissolved. It is a study of a rural society based upon an open-field economy, and though it cannot be called typical in all its aspects, for every community is a unique organism in some way, with its own peculiar flavour and individuality, it may perhaps be regarded as a portrait of the kind of society which existed over a considerable part of central England for the best part of a thousand years.[14]

And if we ask, how could the history of the open-field peasant farmer in one village have represented a contribution to the economic and social history of England?, the answer is straightforward. Wigston Magna was studied steadfastly in the context of those environing *Leicestershire* developments on which Hoskins had worked for two decades previously. The technique here, as elsewhere in his work, was to expand from the particular through thematic comparison and contrast. A settlement might be placed in this wider context by ranking it locally or regionally in terms of size or wealth; a subsequent change in the comparable rank order would then indicate relative changes in prosperity for which reasons had to be sought. Farming methods could be analysed through comparing incidences of crops and livestock. Similarly, occupational groups, be they farmers, clergy, butchers or, in another of Hoskins's studies, great merchants, also might be understood through this comparative technique.[15] On a wider canvas, selected urban economies could be contrasted by comparing whole occupational categories in different towns.[16]

Such historical techniques – and they have continued to be used since, by this author amongst others – certainly helped to highlight the variegated experiences of particular places, and they helped too to give some indication that a settlement undergoing specific investigation reflected some more widely shared development. If Wigston Magna was thus representative of open-field economies in Leicestershire, by common consent a characteristic region of common-field farming, then *ipso facto* the newly drawn corrective picture of such practices in Wigston could be taken by generalist historians as broadly representative of open-field farming economies across the country as a whole. The wider implications for national generalization were thus first hinted at by the author on a highly regionalized basis, and then absorbed into the broader canon of historical thinking.

But if such processes of acceptance helped – as fundamentally they did – to lend respectability to the 'new' local history, it is only possible to understand the significance of subsequent developments in the subject by emphasizing the nature of the comparative technique at this level. First, the starting-point for each comparison was usually a group of individual settlements (or an occupational grouping). Second, the comparisons tended to be made on the basis of single thematic measures – population, wealth, occupation – and were consequently heavily weighted towards 'economic' considerations. Third, such comparisons, insofar as they had to be based initially on relative indices of wealth or population at some point or brief period in the history of a region, tended to be static, the framework of change being assessed through the comparison of two chronologically separate 'static' analyses that were based usually on taxation or ecclesiastical records or upon temporal groupings of probate inventories or of the entries in freemen's rolls. Fourth, and above all, the communal units for comparison in the countryside, being county-based, were then contrasted with those in counties in other regions: the 'communities' of Leicestershire thus became representative of the Lowland Zone, and those of Devon were taken to reflect the Highland Zone. In the case of urban economies, the selection of towns depended initially on the availability of comparable urban records in a group of such centres in neighbouring counties – Leicester, Northampton and Coventry – but with further towns of similar or other 'rank' also drawn into the argument. In all these four instances, then, we return to an earlier point with regard to the relation between local and national history: the connection between the two levels was suggested from selective premises that were then related to some but not all the regions or towns of the country. From this point of view, therefore, the initial influence of the new local history on national interpretation was, and – in the then contexts of record availability and the historiographical climate – could only be, based on the extension of fertile or provocative suggestion from particular areas of the country either to similar areas or types of settlement elsewhere or, more generally, to England as a whole. More precisely, this process led to the sophistication of historical generalization about certain themes in the past of England as a whole. A distance between local history *per se* and national history thus could be, and was, apparently sustained.

It was, of course, a distance that immediately proved in some senses illusory. A mode of expanding an historical theme from the particular to the general, by virtue of a gigantic intellectual leap from the one to the other, simply could not be upheld without the establishment of at least a few nationally contextual frameworks not only with regard to the relative rankings of regions or of towns, but also in respect of the origins or destinies of particular settlements – essential themes of the so-called Leicester School. In this historiographical process of building continuously upwards from local levels to the national, a third major figure, M. W. Beresford, made his appearance from Leeds. With the addition of his weighty advocacy, the 'nationalization' of certain localized themes forced itself on wider attention. A few examples taken in periodic, as opposed to historiographical, sequence must suffice. Through his pioneering examination of all places in the country known as Charlton or Carlton, for instance, Finberg was able to mount an attack on yet another tenet of Anglo-Saxon scholarship, the status of the free peasant or *ceorl*.[17] Similarly, it was partly out of Finberg's systematic analyses of the origins of the towns of Devon and Gloucestershire that there later emerged that invaluable *Handlist* of English medieval boroughs by him and Beresford.[18] But it was Beresford who systematically first raised the analysis of certain urban origins to a national level in his massive study, *New Towns of the Middle Ages*.[19] Moreover, if Hoskins had sought both to rank the wealth of the counties in medieval England and to order at least the leading towns in the early sixteenth century, it was Beresford (and C. A. F. Meekings) who collaborated with Hoskins over the ranking-tables for the leading 42 towns at various points between 1334 and 1861 in *Local History in England*.[20] Most dramatic of all for the growing acceptance of local history was Beresford's own expansion to a national level of the theme of the 'lost village'.[21] It was appropriate that this raising of local themes, and especially those with a topographical slant, to a countrywide significance should find expression both in Beresford's categorized approach to the landscapes of medieval England as seen from the air,[22] and in Hoskins's classic survey of *The Making of the English Landscape* (1955).

Fundamentally important as was this process of 'nationalizing' local history, it was not, and could not be, intended to do more than demonstrate that certain localized experiences were broadly shared across much of the country, and to explain why. It was an essential demonstration in the context of an evolving subject and its wider academic acceptance, but it was local history *per se* in Finberg's sense only insofar as it helped to assert, in a generalized way, some of the basic temporal phases that distinguished the particularized chronological experiences of communities from the overall rhythms of national history. The problems explored still tended to be thematic rather than synthetical; economic and topographical rather than societal (except by implication). The solutions proposed were rightly regarded as contributions to a new understanding of national trends through the multiplication of particular cases. For that purpose, single settlements might be dis-aggregated from their regional settings, and then re-aggregated at a national level according to generalized categories defined by stages in settlement life-cycles from origins to desertion. The service so rendered to local historians was invaluable: national yardsticks against which more detailed local analyses might be measured comparatively were securely drawn; topography as an analytical tool was made respectable even in the eyes of chair-bound historians. Despite such advances, however, they did not solve, nor were they intended to solve, the underlying problem of how localities might be related to the nation as a whole.

If the mode of generalization had to proceed from single communities, then the type of settlement to be most easily fitted into a national framework was the town. Towns, however, were classifiable at either the regional or the national level in terms that might transcend the nature of their various origins or their relative positions as defined by some single measure like size or wealth. Pre-industrialized cities or towns were to be characterized not only in terms of their economic functions, like industry or marketing, but also according to their administrative or social significances *in relation to* some surrounding region or area – whether a 'province', a county, or some smaller marketing area – of which they were then to be seen as centres. With but minor modifications and additions, this qualitative form of categorization, as most influentially employed by Hoskins, has provided the model for comparative urban studies down to the present day, not least in the creative hands of Professor Peter Clark and Dr Paul Slack.[23] This continuing tendency to study single towns in the restricted context of their comparative situation in the hierarchy, as opposed to the interaction between towns at all levels of the hierarchy within or even beyond a region, however, still means that generalization about 'the urban system' at the national level remains locked into a similar kind of analytical discontinuity between the local and the national as that already identified earlier.

It is clear nevertheless that the continuing refinement of classifications based on function, in both urban and agrarian contexts, remains a crucial element in the development of academic local history as a subject with implications wider than the specific. For the countryside, labels based on economic functions take at least a preliminary step towards identifying leading characteristics by which settlements may be usefully differentiated and then compared across the nation. Various writers, for example, have drawn attention to rural settlement-types that relate to communications, whether by road, river, canal or rail; to medieval trading centres in the countryside which had lost their marketing functions; to specialist industrial settlements devoted to cloth-working or metal-working, for instance, from the Middle Ages onwards, and whether characterized by domestic workshops or factory or mill; to settlements evolved around the extraction industries, whether quarrying or mining; to 'intensive farming' settlements; to different forms of fishing village; and to more specific forms of occupational sub-community concerned with the inland waterways.[24] (To this plethora of types, finally perhaps, may be added that of the idealistic community: settlements or colonies contrived by the persecuted or the dedicated minority group like the Quakers or the Chartists.[25])

Such labels undoubtedly represent an advance on regional rankings of settlements by size or wealth, but their very proliferation militates increasingly against a structured view of how congeries of communities under a type-heading may be taken in any period to comprise more than a collective illustration of some broadly experienced socio-economic trend at a national level of generalization. As they stand, the underlying similarities between two or more *different* types are obscured: the label usually describes but one feature of what eventually has been accomplished rather than indicating some local factor or factors conducive to that accomplishment – the major exception here being the erstwhile rural market centre, the characteristics of which have been shown unambiguously to have influenced subsequent developments. Had not two further approaches to the problem of categorization been evolved already in the 1960s, therefore, the classificatory approach itself might now be facing a form of analytical stalemate.

The closer of these two new approaches to the more established methods of classification, in that it was concerned wholly with the typification of single rural townships, was that based on the old poor-law distinction between 'open' and 'closed' settlements. The systematic construction of a whole spectrum of types between these two extremes over the last 20 years or so, however, owes most to Dr Dennis R. Mills,[26] who in his recent volume, *Lord and Peasant in Nineteenth Century Britain* (1980), has pursued the subject to a point where he feels able to claim that this form of categorization has some of the force of a predictive model.[27] Not only may this type of categorization have some explanatory as opposed to labelling value, therefore, but as a system of classification it purports to be societal, rather than economic or functional. While proceeding from a single premise – the presence or absence of a dominant estate in any one settlement – it then combines bundles of characteristics such as population size, class structure, occupational diversity, degrees of poverty, quality of housing, varying tendencies towards order or disorder, and religious propensities. The resulting spectrum of settlement-types – as it emerges in the hands of different scholars – now ranges from estate villages and absentee landlord villages, via 'divided parishes' of both substantial and small landholders, to freeholder townships (some of which were earlier market villages) and squatter settle-ments.[28] Its great merit as a multi-dimensional system of characterization is that at the level of national historical generalization it helps to break down the crude divisions of the nation by broadly sketched social 'classes' into something approaching different types of inter-related reality on the ground and on an internally consistent continuum.

Methodologically the 'open'/'closed' dichotomy is most applicable from the late seventeenth century onwards, though its study has so far been largely restricted to the nineteenth century, when comparable data is widely available for most parishes and by when the pattern of landholding on which the classification depends had long been determined. To that limited extent then, this form of the categorization resembles the economic-function label: in essence it describes an already accomplished state by that late period. Furthermore, to be nationally applicable, it too depends ultimately on the multiplication of cases, township by township, and in a manner that is largely independent of regional variation and, indeed – despite its specifically sociological bias – independent of those wider structures of a political, administrative or socio-economic kind that helped the society of a county, for example, at one level to cohere and at another to integrate with the wider society of the nation. Like all such systems of classification so far discussed, it is a tool that may be used to build upwards towards a higher level of understanding.

The second of the two new approaches to rural categorization began from a basically different premise in that instead of working upwards from individual settlements, the classification worked downwards. It evolved with the realiz-ation that in the countryside there was a further identifiable spatial level of analysis which was wider than that of the particular community but more restricted in scope than, for example, a county area: the farming region. The study of farming regions, of course, was not new,[29] but it is fair to say that it was only with the sequence of studies produced by Dr Joan Thirsk that the subject came to be treated systematically as a matter of more than purely agricultural or manorial interest. It was a sequence that ran, *inter alia*, through from her 1953 Occasional Paper on fenland farming via her major comparative study of all the regions of Lincolnshire in 1957 to her national survey of farming regions in *The Agrarian History of England and Wales, IV, 1500–1640* in 1967 – a landmark in the sophistication of rural historical studies.[30] It was a sequence that was weightily and independently paralleled by Professor Eric Kerridge's work on Wiltshire and the country generally for the more specific purpose of charting the early progress of agricultural improvement.[31] By 1967, the relevance of the farming region to a whole range of other themes could no longer be ignored by economic and social historians.

For out of what ostensibly might seem to have been a preoccupation with such matters as field-systems, cropping, stock-raising, enclosure and the like, now emerged a new approach to the wider study of society. In taking up and refashioning a theme which was first analysed by Tupling a generation earlier on a restricted regional basis, for the purposes of her seminal essay 'Industries in the Countryside',[32] Joan Thirsk sketched out what today seems to be developing, despite the author's disclaimer of this as her intention, into nothing less than a powerful explanatory 'model' of rural socio-economic development; in the breadth of its applicability, at least, it is probably as close to the status of a model as an historical analysis may reach. It was a framework of explanation that has been influentially reinforced and expanded in a series of studies by Professor Alan Everitt which have pursued new themes both forward into the nineteenth century and backwards to the days of settlement.[33] In the process, what began as an agriculturally defined region has been transmuted into a geographical conception of different kinds of distinctive countryside or *pays* like the Cotswolds, the Lincolnshire Fens, or the Kentish Weald – each with its own more or less typical history and social *persona*. The result has been not only a logical extension of Hoskins's and Finberg's concern to relate historic landscapes to their inhabitants, but also the creation of a new and sophisticated means of comparing entire localities of similar type in different parts of the country. No longer artificially contained by county boundaries, many of which are straddled by stretches of relatively homogeneous countryside, local historians had identified a method by which local societies might be related to the wider social development of the country as a whole. With this advance and its nation-wide applicability, academic 'local history' might with reason be more properly characterized as 'English local history'.

The countrysides of England are many and various, but with the work of Thirsk and Everitt a degree of broad categorization became possible. Above all, attention was refocused, away from the text-book dimensions of classic open-field farming areas, and onto a variety of equally significant, but thereto largely ignored, areas of pastoral farming. It was a division of the country which was not restricted to the distinction between Highland Zone and Lowland Zone, important as that still remained, but which also took account of the pastoral economies and societies within lowland England itself. As a result, it has become possible for Alan Everitt provisionally to suggest:

a broad classification into eight types or categories of countryside: the fielden or 'champion' areas, the forest areas, the fell or moorland areas, the fenlands, the

marshlands, the heathlands, the downlands, and the wold or *wald* countrysides.
These categories are only rough and ready ones; at many points they clearly overlap;
and they must not be thought of as either rigid in their boundaries or unchanging in
their character over the centuries. No classification can be altogether satisfactory,
and a number of further subdivisions might obviously be suggested.[34]

The temporal reservations expressed here are very important: indeed, what
makes this approach so relevant is its accommodation to the historical process.
The areas and the characters of *pays* may be subject to eventual transformation:
woodland, for example, may be gradually superseded by open pasture, and
open pasture may in its turn be converted into arable. Nevertheless, it is now
equally apparent that the characteristics of more slowly changing different
countrysides were continuous over many centuries as a direct result of when
and how they were shaped at the times of their settlement. In Everitt's more
recent work on Kent in particular, stress is placed on the implications of the
connected patterns laid down respectively in different kinds of countryside in
the very earliest stages of settlement, in the mid to late-Saxon period, in the late
Anglo-Saxon and early medieval periods, in the sixteenth and early seventeenth centuries, and in the eighteenth and nineteenth centuries.[35] Such
patterns embrace not only the contrasted siting of settlements and their forms –
whether nucleated or dispersed – their field-system, their types of farming, but
also such differing characteristics as parish size, degrees of manorialization and
variations of social structure. On whether the local societies most characteristic
of different *pays* emerged at one level as estate or open parish communities,
depended their ability or inability to control subsequent local population
growth, with all the implications that that often brought with it, in terms of the
need to develop alternative sources of income to agriculture in the shape of
by-employments – handicraft or extractive industries in many pastoral areas,
service trades in some felden areas – let alone the problems of poverty, and the
propensity to protest against the invasion of customary rights.[36] The inhabitants of the different *pays* might be distinguished in other ways too. Where
manorialization was weak, especially in pastoral areas, the proliferation of
smallholders and cottage-farmers with reasonably assured tenures engendered
a shared and sturdy sense of independence and personal freedom which might
find expression in various types of religious nonconformity or even, it has
recently been argued, in local political attitudes during the seventeenth
century.[37]

This major historiographical advance in the subject led to a distinct shift in the
ways in which English local historians viewed the wider nature of their
discipline. Not only might individual rural communities now be seen as more
precise expressions of their contexts than had been the case, but primacy might
be accorded to these new contexts. Instead of local community, the new
emphasis could be on regional societies and their contrasting rates of evolution.
As Alan Everitt has stated:

It seems to me that it is impossible to understand the historical development of
this country at all unless we recognize this fact: unless we admit that until recently
England has never been a monolithic community but an incomplete amalgam of
differing but related societies, of differing but related *pays*.[38]

What is significant here, for present purposes, is that the frame of reference within which the investigation of such entities might take place is clearly that of English society as a whole. The society of the *pays* might be regarded as 'a distinct articulation' of national society, but at the same time the whole society is to be seen as an amalgam of such smaller societies and their more recently emergent rivals – the industrial areas and, later still, 'the growing scale of regional capitals, and their growing influence over their hinterlands or dependent regions'.[39] Instead of building up to a national level through the multiplication of particularized classes of community, here was a local·historical approach that embraced a coherent vision of the national society as the product of its distinctive parts.

Paradoxically, despite this wider vision, the *pays* has rarely been studied in such contexts. The inter-penetration of contrasting *pays* – the river valleys, the wolds and the Weald of Kent – has been analysed for the earliest periods,[40] but the manner in which the societies of *pays* in later times may have been inter-connected, and often superseded by, or absorbed to some extent into regions of industrialization or into the hinterlands of great towns, has not. There is not yet even a systematic study of the relation of the society of an important market town situated between, and mediating between, two contrasting *pays*, and the societies of the two *pays* in question. On the contrary, there has been a tendency for the *pays* to become another example of the local historical 'horizon' – an upper cut-off point beyond which local historians rarely venture. Certainly *pays* may be compared and contrasted in different regions of the country, but there is also a sense in which the national perspective is being obscured. The main emphasis has been in the opposite direction: on the ways in which the *pays* itself has helped to characterize the component rural communities within it. Thus Joan Thirsk's broad survey of the sixteenth and early seventeenth centuries entailed 'an enumeration of the basic farming systems of England's different regions . . . and an analysis of the types of community associated with each'.[41] At a greater level of detail, moreover, we now have important published studies from various viewpoints of communities in clayland 'felden' areas, in woodland areas (one in a royal forest, the other not), in fen or fen-edge areas, and in a chalk countryside.[42]

In one sense, therefore, the *pays* concept has interposed a new local historical frame of reference between the individual settlement and the country as a whole. Within the *pays*, socio-economic processes, or even the spread of religious dissent, are measured not only in relation to national trends but more particularly in relation to the internal development of that *pays* as a whole. Stress is placed on the investigation of the possible salient characteristics by which one *pays* may be differentiated from another, and on the reasons why different types of countryside appear to have evolved so divergently. The mode of community classification is relational: relational to a countryside in the same way as towns may be related to their variously characterizable surrounding areas. Equally, in the same way as towns at different points in such an urban hierarchy may be compared in different regions, so too, theoretically, may be rural communities from similar *pays* in different parts of the country. Alternatively, as in Margaret Spufford's invaluable community study, communities within three different types of countryside (as well as specifically within a wider county context), may be fruitfully contrasted in order to test a variety of local responses to more general trends like the decline of the small landowner, education and patterns of religious allegiance.[43] Most ambitious of all is Victor Skipp's attempt to relate five townships with dispersed populations in the forest of Arden to such major problems as the Malthusian check and even the 'General European Crisis' of the seventeenth century.[44] The *pays* and its constituent communities may thus be seen on the one hand as a potential building block towards the further understanding of the wider society (although, since it has yet to be used as such, the study of it tends to be internalized); and on the other hand, as in the case of earlier community studies, as a test-bed for the examination of general historical processes. A pattern, then, will be now becoming familiar to the reader: English local historians frequently tend to look inwards when it comes to structures, and outwards when it comes to thematic processes. Except insofar as each may be likened to comparable entities elsewhere, the community or even the society of the *pays*, it would seem, stands sturdily alone, untethered in an unkind world, and buffeted by cold winds of change that occasionally rise to galeforce.

One solution to the problems and limitations of studying single entities – be they rural or urban – is strongly urged by one modern school of local historical thought.[45] It is that the diversity of the provincial experience is best integrated within, and illuminated by, the overall study of a region. Within a region, towns and trade and industry may, for example, be related to agriculture, society and communications in a satisfying whole; while the region as some sort of entity helps to expand the object of the local historical enquiry from possibly unrepresentative, and often insufficiently documented, single communities to a point where more real contact is made with the local society of which such communities were, after all, but a part. There is much to be said for this point of view. In the hands of experts like Dr J. D. Marshall, regional studies have contributed fundamentally to the progress of our understanding. More than that, the study of areas smaller than the region is made immeasurably more profitable when securely placed within an already researched regional context. Whether 'regional history' helps to solve the problem of the local historical horizon, however, is another matter.

'The region' as a unit of investigation normally turns out to be a county (or, for example, the Lake counties), the longest and most firmly established object of local historical study. In recent times, moreover, it has been studied in ways that are almost as various as its historians. At one extreme the writing of its history remains the classic type of local history *per se* in the best modern sense of that term. Hoskins's own study of Devon from prehistory to the present; Bouch and Jones's work on the Lake counties since c. 1500; and Chalklin's book on seventeenth-century Kent: all these are concerned essentially with regional explanation in the round (but with particular emphasis on socio-economic matters) and for its own sake.[46] It is left to the reader to draw such wider implications as he may wish, and such studies are none the worse for that.

More outward looking, secondly, are those analyses that treat more fully also of religious and political processes that thematically transcend the region under discussion. This approach, so brilliantly pioneeered by A. L. Rowse in his marvellously evocative 'portrait of a society' in Tudor Cornwall, seeks deliberately to treat of a province as a microcosm of the whole society especially during periods of substantial change like the sixteenth and seventeenth centuries.[47] While each such author may emphasize particular themes for investigation – religious radicalism, Tawney's century, the societal implications of the shift away from medieval traditions[48] – the central intention is to relate provincial change to national change on a wide variety of fronts. As such, therefore, this approach represents 'national history localized' *par excellence*. It is hardly surprising that it is usually practised by those who would not necessarily regard themselves as local historians.

More sharply distinguished by its delineation of the relation of the county to central government has been a third group of county studies which owes much to the earlier views of Neale and Namier on the nature of the English polity as in some sense resembling a confederation of county commonwealths. This approach, so profoundly influenced by Alan Everitt's pioneering work, *The Community of Kent and the Great Rebellion 1640–60* (1966), began by inspecting the relations between province and nation at the point of break-down, but it has been ably pursued backwards in time to embrace not only the earlier seventeenth century in Cheshire and Sussex, but also Elizabethan Norfolk, Tudor and Stuart Kent generally, and more recently various counties in the later Middle Ages.[49]

It has been this approach – for all that it has its detractors[50] – which has most closely linked local and national history. The minute dissection of the provincial governing classes and spill-over of their activities onto the national stage, and conversely, to take but one example, 'the changing relationship between the London government and the County of Kent',[51] has led to a general re-interpretation of periods building up to the mid-seventeenth-century national crisis and even beyond. That said, however, the objects of analysis most usually reflect the local history of the *political* nation. Analyses that simultaneously take the political story down to the levels of town, *pays* or village are rare indeed.[52] It should be emphasized, nonetheless, that the deeper potential of comparative county studies is already there to be realized. The varying incidence of noble and gentry estates from county to county that is being increasingly established as a fundamental feature not only of the seventeenth, but also of the nineteenth century,[53] may yet be linked, for example, to the patterns of strong and weak manorialization in different *pays*; and to the contrasted county distributions of 'open' and 'closed' townships.

The county as something rather more than an administrative entity has also been illuminated from another angle, that of the county town: whether this be regarded either as a centre of administration, of marketing – with transport links to the peripheries of the shire – of nascent craft regions, of specialist services, or of social and cultural life generally and for the gentry in particular; or as a focus for immigration.[54] It has perhaps been unfortunate, therefore, that the division of much current local historical writing into areas covered respectively by either urban or agrarian historians has meant that shire and county town have rarely been analysed together. Closer attention has been paid to the relation between towns, either further up or lower down the urban hierarchy, and their surrounding regions. Most so-called regional histories certainly remain county-based yet, in them, town and country tend to be treated quite separately and with little regard to the fact that neither urban fields nor agricultural regions were necessarily confined by county boundaries. To this extent, then, the hope of regional historians that urban and rural societies might be analytically integrated has yet to be realized.

We return inevitably to the problem of the local historical horizon. Presumably because of difficulty of access to documentary repositories rather than for theoretical reasons, local historians rarely look beyond the limits of a county, except when relations with central government are involved. Nor are they alone in this: generalist historians have often been equally reluctant to venture beyond such boundaries in order to study noble and gentry landholding and influence, for example. In the case of the English local historian in particular, this failure might seem to be particularly illogical, given the slowly changing stance of his subject. For always in the background of this discussion there has lain a fundamental historiographical shift: a shift from a perspective that looked upwards and outwards from the local community, to a different viewpoint, from which local historians in practice now tend to look downwards and inwards from the perspective of either the *pays* or that of the county region, to the different types of community within them. If the latter is the more true perspective for the local historian to adopt, then he may have to allow also for a viewpoint superior yet: from a still wider territorial standpoint such as 'the North'. It is noticeable that ground of this nature is more usually traversed by other than local historians.[55]

This survey of the wider concerns of English local history began with a dilemma apparently inherent in the practice of the subject: a tension between the opposing gravitational pulls of local history *per se* on the one hand and of 'national history localized' on the other. The evolution of the discipline in the 35 years since Finberg first enunciated its aims, however, has shown this dilemma in some sense to have been false. Local history *per se*, in Finberg's meaning of the term, has been 'nationalized'; 'national history localized' has been replaced, at least partially, by frames of reference that are intermediate between nation and community, and in ways that Finberg could not have foreseen when first he spoke on the subject. That said, most academic local historians are still bent on identifying, and/or suggesting solutions to, newly perceived general processes at local levels. The real dilemma, then, is between the genius of a place – or district – which is usually analysed selectively for these over-riding purposes, and the trends or changes that may be shown by the comparative technique to be of a more general significance. In such cases, there is a sense of building up from the singular (and indeed often at its expense) to some higher order of understanding, a sense of movement towards national levels, yet what that higher order of understanding might be is rarely defined in terms more general than the regionalized variation of the 'national' processes or problems which each local historian chooses to address in his micro-study. Where it has been defined, this larger question has not been systematically explored.

Chapter 2

Local History: The Need for a Framework

There are many different ways of studying and writing local history. But some ways are to my mind more profitable than others. . .

(W.G. Hoskins, *Local History in England*, 1959, p.3)

While the relationsip between local history and national history has undoubtedly altered over the last 35 years, it cannot be claimed that the essence of that relationship is understood very much more precisely now than it was in 1952. The purposes of English local history, indeed, continue to be constrained – at a wider variety of levels, perhaps – by tacitly agreed local historical horizons and never more so than when comparisons are drawn between two or more such 'bounded' local worlds. But if the inhabitants of places or districts are to be seen as more than social reflections of their immediate urban and rural environments, as more than vehicles for wider historical change, how should they be viewed? If classification may hardly be regarded as an end in itself, what is the end which it is intended to serve? If local historians currently tend to deal in somewhat confined and isolated structures which are basically connected to the world beyond the region only by virtue of the fact that they are taken to exemplify supra-regional processes, how else might these structures be seen to integrate with that wider setting? If we *could* so connect them, regardless of the conventional horizons, are there ways conversely in which we might still preserve some sense of the individual provincial genius of each such society? In doing that, might we not also begin to seek ways rather different from the methods we adopt at present, by which to compare past local realities: that is, not simply by comparing similar societies in parallel, but by comparing them according to their contrasted individual relationships to a conceptualized national framework? Could we but attempt this, a more precise integration of local and national history than is presently the case might become possible.

There are many reasons, both recent and current, why English local historians now might seek to identify a generalized overall framework that is sufficiently flexible for them to be able to work within it towards some shared and broadly apprehended end. The first and most fundamental reason is that, by the very nature of the subject, there is a need for an ever-increasing number of geographically and thematically diversified findings to be brought together into some conceptually coherent inter-relationship. The very absence of such a framework indeed might seem to raise serious questions about the distinctiveness of the subject as an academic discipline, questions that are underlined, as we shall see, by the nature of the wider historiographical trends in which English local history has evolved and is still evolving.

The second reason is that academic local historians have always worked within frameworks of one kind or another, and there seems no justification for ceasing to do so now. To some of these earlier frameworks, allusion has already been made. There is the peculiar chronological framework within which the life-cycles of local communities are now seen. There is the framework provided by the geographical regions and sub-regions of England, a framework that in different ways has ever lain behind the most illuminating local historical writing and which still marks the more influential accounts of provincial diversity, especially at the level of the *pays*. There is also that framework of humane economic history that owes so much to the example of R. H. Tawney, and which, until quite recently, dominated the thematic concerns of those analysing both rural and urban societies. Most characteristic of all is that framework which became the early hall-mark of the Leicester School, a framework which sought successfully to integrate the facts of topography with socio-economic trends, to a point where anyone properly trained in this tradition is now able to begin to read the outline history even of an unfamiliar English region from the evidence of its landscape.

With, thirdly, the broadening of local historical concerns since the 1960s, however, it is arguable that the established frameworks are no longer sufficiently comprehensive also to embrace the new range of interests with its growing emphasis on social and cultural matters. Looming more prominently than ever before are such themes as population and family, kinship and neighbourhood, education and religion, ritual and superstition. If 'economic man', who once dominated local historical reconstructions of the past, has now been replaced by 'man the sentient being', who also worshipped, read and held political views, so too has the more rounded, integrated study of past local societies been proved to be possible. Such 'communities', be they rural or urban, are now being seen increasingly as socially constituted and socially functioning entities within the wider ambit of socio-economic contexts and change.[1] The absence of a containing sociological frame of reference within which such studies might be situated, however, is most marked.

If the need for a new overall framework for English local history may be urged for the three reasons given, there is also a fourth factor. Without a conceptual framework peculiar to the subject, its identity as a disciplined field of study may become less distinctive. This is a new problem that has arisen out of the general historiographical efflorescence which has marked the last 25 years. Areas of investigation which local history had itself fostered have since in their turn inclined towards ever greater specialization in their own rights. In the visual field, it is only necessary to recall the growing sophistication and coverage of the field archaeologists; the highly specialized developments in, for example, vernacular architecture and, more recently, industrial archaeology. There is even a new breed of landscape historian. In terms of man's relation to his environment, there are now spatial analyses by historical geographers and, from demographers, statistical approaches of extraordinary subtlety. There is working-class history, women's history and oral history, let alone a growing field of folk-life studies. On a yet wider canvas, but in contexts immediately germane to the local historian's concerns, it needs to be re-emphasized that there have emerged two, virtually separate, fields of study: agrarian history (especially agricultural history) and urban history, the personnel involved in each of which only partially overlap. Above all, in every one of these areas of inquiry – and in others too – there has been an increasing tendency for scholars who would not necessarily wish to call themselves local historians to take a locality or a 'community' as a kind of laboratory in which to test a theory or a wide-ranging specialist theme like illegitimacy or crime. Even such roundly conceived notions as the medieval 'community of the vill' and the early modern rural 'community' have been dissected by sociologically-minded general historians.[2] At first sight, it might seem that the concerns of academic local historians, who themselves tend to emphasize some themes before others, and those of the generalist historians who are concerned less with national affairs than with national themes at local levels, have merged to such a point that the differences between them are now barely distinguishable.

If the need for some sort of fresh theoretical framework against which findings that are peculiar to local historians may be set is scarcely deniable, the nature of that framework must be true to the central purpose of the subject. To recall that, we could do no better than to return to a priority expressed by H. P. R. Finberg. 'The local historian', he wrote, 'should concern himself not with areas as such, but with *social entities* [my italics].'[3] Each of these entities might be described as a 'community', by which Finberg meant 'a set of people occupying an area with defined territorial limits and so far united in thought and action as to feel a sense of belonging together, in contradistinction from the many outsiders who do not belong' – a definition that, broadly interpreted, might embrace not only towns and villages but also the inhabitants of a distinctive *pays* like the Forest of Dean, or even, at one social level, a shire.[4] The implications of this definition are surely fundamental to the situation of English local historical studies in a national historiographical dimension even though Finberg himself, in his desire to demarcate the separate domain of local history, did not pursue the logic of his stated position. We may, however, perhaps agree with him for the moment that the prime focus of local history is people in recognizable 'societies' at levels lower and narrower than that of the nation as a whole. Ideally, local history is societal history; it is not – or should not be, except in a preliminary way – purely thematic, in the sense that it is merely illustrative of an economic, social, demographic, topographical or any other kind of wider historical theme or process; for these are but points of entry into something broader, richer, more humane and ultimately more inclusive. That certainly is what lies behind a number of recent and overtly societal approaches to the study of *pays*, village and town.[5] Indeed it is arguable that now so much of the ground – in both economic and topographical terms – has already been cleared, and that now the tools of the so-called 'new social history' are being increasingly sophisticated, the over-riding concern of English local history should be re-stated boldly.

English local history, as its title declares, should be seen as a specialized branch of the history of our national 'society' in the broadest and most integrated sense of that term. It is the local history of the English, not as a race but as an evolving people, that is the prime object of study. It is not the local history of Eng*land* either as a nation-state or as a physical entity which is then artificially partitioned for the purposes of defining, and then studying, its regional or local parts simply in order to illuminate broad socio-economic trends that consequently tend to disguise what is richly variegated or even unique. It is the social and cultural diversity of the English experience which has yet to be fully understood in the context of, and which has still to be related to, the wider organization of the whole society. If we wished to be technical, we might say that the aims of the English local historian, therefore, should be first to discover and to illuminate the various societal microstructures of the past insofar as these may be broadly associated with districts or places; and second to seek to trace the ever-adjusting symbiosis between these provincial micro-structures and between them and the social and cultural macro-structure of the English nation. In other words, the local historian can afford no longer to subordinate the fact that his objects of study merge into the over-arching framework of national society. From a societal viewpoint in particular, the difference between local history and national history is not only one of subject-matter, it is also one of stance. It is that extra awareness that comes from understanding social realities and social peculiarities in their proper local contexts and, following from that, it is the opportunity to look upwards and outwards *connectively* from the particular to the general, which together should distinguish the stance of the local historian from that of his generalist or thematically inclined colleagues. To this extent, the incursions from 'above' of the specialists into traditional local historical 'territories' in pursuit of purely thematic goals should enhance the distinctiveness of the local historical approach rather than otherwise. Insofar as urban or agrarian historians are concerned with English societal structures, moreover, their fields must represent no more than specialized subdivisions of that wider terrain that is English local history, since it is only in this, or in some similarly inclusive sense – whatever we call it – that a meaningful synthesis of town and country will ever prove feasible.

If this is the essential domain of English local history, the construction of a possible framework in the context of a societal approach will require first that we should glance briefly at the degree to which, and the manner in which, generalist historians are currently concerned with the history of the national society. Only then may we sensibly explore to what extent the local historian's present objects of analysis can be related to such wider frames of reference.

Chapter 3

National Society and Local Societies:
The Quest for Connection

> . . . I believe we should study places, localities, counties, and regions not simply for their own sake, but for the light they shed on English society as a whole.
>
> (Alan Everitt, *Landscape and Community in England*, 1985, p. 9)

Societal history may be defined for present purposes as the history of the component structures of a whole society and the manner in which such structures have been inter-related, both within some simultaneously evolving form of overall social organization, and within that changing climate of ideas which informs and justifies it. In this sense, societal history is neither institutional history nor social history which currently is more concerned with thematic problems ranging from such topics as 'the family' or 'the poor' to crime and witchcraft. It partakes of both these approaches and of others, especially cultural history whether polite or popular, but its chief aim ought to be integrative: to refabricate something of Maitland's 'seamless web'.

This ideal, however, is not one to which many English historians have aspired. Modern French historians may write boldly – perhaps too boldly for our liking – about for example 'L'Identité de la France', but at least they seek to do so synoptically over long historical periods and in a manner that pays due regard to provincial diversity.[1] In this country, where national historical writing is still dominated by thematic approaches – political, religious, economic and so on – and by heavily confined systems of periodization, attempts to synthesize at levels wider and higher than the purely local have been few indeed. For most English historians, Marxian or not, 'social structure' still means class structure alone (and then it is usually described in terms more redolent of an unfilled layer cake), as though the retrospective and hence Whiggish application of a contemporary social obsession in some way helps to explain English society down to its foundations in the past. It is no accident that the over-riding theme which now dominates the writing of social history in this country is the ever-growing 'polarization' of society since 1500. To the inquisitive outsider, indeed, it might even seem that whatever may have been the interlocking structures of English society in the past, it is more than curious that they did not burst asunder long ago.

Nevertheless, there are notable exceptions to these generalized strictures, and it is not irrelevant to note that the historians concerned are all scholars who, having investigated local societies of one shape or another, have then tended to proceed from this perspective towards yet wider integrated surveys. At a national level the broadening of historical understanding, if not necessarily of historical execution, may best be illustrated perhaps by referring on the one hand to A. L. Rowse's *The England of Elizabeth: the structure of society* (1950), and on the other hand to Peter Laslett's interim report on *The World We Have Lost* (1965). The former must represent one of the most remarkable and successful efforts yet to have been attempted to evoke the nature of English society as a whole, from the regional grass-roots upwards during a particular period. The latter, more popular, more restricted in theme, and more sociological in its matter, nevertheless added the family and household to the agenda for discussion, and did so in more socially structured contexts which included a 'local' dimension in the shape of 'community', and which were treated over contrasting time-scales. Two other societal studies, though 'regional', similarly have regard to both the local and the wider forms of social organization in equally different ways: R. H. Hilton's synoptic survey of a poorly documented period, *A Medieval Society: the West Midlands at the end of the thirteenth century* (1966), and Mervyn James's insightful and highly original *Family, Lineage and Civil Society* (1974). More recently still, and thus more in line with the increasingly sociological thinking of the last decade or so, has been a truly notable general study by Dr Keith Wrightson, *English Society 1580–1680* (1982).

That judicious discussion may be accepted perhaps as broadly representative of what appears to be the current mode of thinking with regard to the analysis of English societal structures. In it, three major elements in society are taken to comprise 'the enduring structures' of the social framework: a countrywide system of social differentiation with its cross-cutting ties of patronage and deference; 'the local community' and its neighbourly area; and the household or family with its radiating tentacles of kinship. In this construct, as in others like it, there are two matters that are of immediate concern to the local historian. The first is the undeniably important emphasis that is laid on 'community' as part of the overall framework. The second is a question arising from this first point: how, in 'sociological' terms, may we relate a multitude of individual rural or urban communities to English society as a whole? Must we leap conceptually from a myriad more or less reconstructable realities on the ground to a generalized model of 'community' that in its turn is then related to the other two structures, or is there some other way?

The family, it is true, is usually taken as the basic unit both of community and of society; the 'community', equally, may be regarded as tied to the national mode of social classification not only through its own social subdivisions but also often through its manorial links with the wider estates of the nobility or gentry; yet at a more concrete level of analysis, 'community', unlike both 'family' and 'class', relates – in the accepted commonsense meaning of the term – to a specific area. It is also of a more variegated character, comprising as it does both families *and* classes and many other qualities. To be logical, 'community' – as a spatial expression of social relations – should be linked to yet higher orders of spatially definable social relations until such ascending orders of relations may be taken eventually to comprehend the whole society. If, in structural terms, such higher orders are to be identified only in one dimension, that of 'class', then we might be forced back – over many centuries – on the restricted social context of the so-called 'county community' of nobility and gentry as the next possible spatial layer of interaction. Rightly, however, this is not an option that is suggested by historians since it is difficult to see such a forum for a single 'class' (insofar as it is agreed to have been one) as forming part of a spatial continuum of social relations stretching upwards and outwards from the local community to the nation. Nor, in sociological terms, may the gap be bridged by falling back on other forms of explanation like 'the unification of the realm' (which is invariably accelerated by political historians) or the centralizing apparatuses of church and state; the development of inter-regional trade (which tends to be retarded by economic historians); the ever-growing importance of London and of other major urban centres; the insidious spread of a 'unifying' national culture (which again is usually accelerated, this time by social historians); and so on.

If there is a key to this socio-spatial problem, it is surely to be sought first at those levels of historical analysis that are the usual objects of local historical investigation. To what extent then does the current study of past local societies help us to build up from the ground towards an understanding of yet wider spatial expressions of social relations? If such objects of study prove not to help us directly in this quest, then clearly it will be necessary to examine other possibilities that might well prove to be already implicit in some of the former if we approached them differently. We must return therefore to certain problems surrounding community studies; to the questions posed by the concept of the *pays*; to the influence of marketing centres; and, since the 'county community' seems to be disqualified from inclusion in this survey for reasons given, to the validity of the 'region' in the present context. In doing so, it should become clear that as in the case of local historical approaches to socio-economic processes, there appear to be but two alternative responses to the central sociological question: how do we relate community to society? Either we start from a 'community' and work outwards from it in some increasing spatial sense, and then 'hop' thematically to some borrowed perception of the wider society; or we begin with a region or a countryside and work down to its constituent 'communities'. In both cases, there is inevitably an upper cut-off point that is defined by the limitations of the local historical horizon on the one hand; and a gulf that separates that cut-off point from the wider interests of generalist historians, most of whom give overwhelming precedence to the 'class' factor, on the other. The problems to be discussed, then, are problems shared by both local *and* generalist historians.

In exploring this fundamental problem of how to connect 'communities' to higher orders of social organization, a first point that should be made relates to the technique of categorization and comparison. At this level of analysis, the comparison of classified single settlements clearly becomes irrelevant as a starting-point (even though it should still prove instructive at a later stage of examination). Nowhere, perhaps, is this clearer than in the context of the 'open'/ 'closed' typology (in which there tends anyway to be an uncomfortably large undefinable residual category) which, as a modern conceptual technique, now masks the very elements of inter-parochial social inter-relationship that it was formerly intended to highlight. The original contemporary distinction between 'open' and 'closed' was based on inter-township comparison with regard to the supply of labour. As has been sensibly pointed out, 'a meaningful definition of a "close" parish must be a place so restricted in the settlement of wage-dependent families that the supply of labour was insufficient for the cultivation of its area' – i.e., it had to import labour on an annual or seasonal basis. 'An "open" parish was one in which labour was surplus to need, and which provided additional manpower for the neighbourhood.' On this definition, attempts to characterize villages by intra-parochial land-holding patterns alone are doomed to failure. Many places that may be categorized on this property basis as 'closed' already had a sufficiency of resident labour and did not, therefore, need to import it from elsewhere. By contrast, many villages other than closed villages were deficient in cottages and so did have to import labour.[2] In other words, the documentary difficulties involved in elucidating labour-supply patterns should not be allowed to cause us to forget that, on this single measure alone (quite apart from the others that may have flowed from it, such as the personal contacts that led to marriage), townships require to be studied in relation to each other and probably also to local market centres.

Another approach which starts from the single community but which deliberately works outwards from it has been inspired by the example of the rural sociologist W. M. Williams, who was able to define variously delimited and often overlapping patterns of external social contacts which went to make up a community's 'social area'.[3] As Dr Margaret Spufford has stated in what has rightly become a classic community study:

> The ideal basis for a study of this kind would not be a number of contrasting village communties, but a number of contrasting neighbourhoods or 'social areas', each extending over a group of parishes within approximately an eight-mile radius of a focal village centre.[4]

With the idea of 'neighbourhoods' it is impossible not to concur. There is evidence from every direction for interconnections between proximate parishes brought about by supra-parochial land-holding or by patterns of physical mobility, of inter-marriage, and of the supra-parochial memberships of early non-conforming congregations, to name but a few such links. In the case of Keith Wrightson's Terling the range of a sample of such contacts has been clearly mapped, and over an even wider area than an eight-mile radius.[5]

Yet in the context of the issue under discussion (as opposed to the perfectly proper terms of restricted reference within which the protagonists of this concept speak), there are conceptual difficulties. First, it is not at all clear whether the links in question are strictly communal or strictly individual: what we really need to know, therefore, is either how *many* individuals are involved in the links between particular places, or which links should be given priority in the definition of such an area. Secondly, and assuming that broadly equal quantities of evidence for reciprocal relationships could be derived from surrounding, more or less proximate, communities, how would we define the density of links that go to delimit one such neighbourhood from another? Where in fact do we end when a whole series of overlapping social areas radiating outwards from numbers of variously sized communities is involved? I suspect that to be quite sure of our ground, it would be necessary to probe well beyond the proposed eight-mile limit in each case (and so perhaps *ad infinitum*). In perhaps a majority of instances at this point, thirdly, there is bound to arise the problem of a rival focus, especially that of the town. For the sake of argument only we may perhaps leave to one side the attractive powers of the widely spaced major regional centres: what surely should concern us here is the influence of the local market town.

The impact of the local market centre cannot be underestimated: unpublished research shows unambiguously the ways in which such little towns as Lutterworth and Melton Mowbray in Leicestershire exerted a developing economic influence from the sixteenth century onwards at the latest over their agrarian hinterlands, and in the process thereby helped to give a character to the areas affected through the impulses for agricultural improvement and marketing that emanated from or through them.[6] In contrasted areas which were not so biased originally towards mixed farming, the market town of the eighteenth century in particular might assume a different role as the centre of what Professor Alan Everitt has dubbed an 'occupational' or 'craft region', whether, for example, that was devoted to shoe-making or lace-making or to the straw-plait industry.[7] Whatever the case, some social connections will have flowed from the economic links which attached a semi-industrialized rural community to its nearest small town. Most such towns will certainly have been *foci* for migration at least from the areas so dominated by them. Through them, as well as through towns in more agriculturally biased areas, moreover, the local agricultural labour force was circulated via the mechanism of the hiring fair. In the nineteenth century, it is even possible to characterize the distinctive patterns of rural-urban connection through the reconstruction of carriers' routes focusing on urban market centres, and thereby to define, often with some precision, what appear to have been the sometimes clearly demarcated but limited socio-economic hinterlands of certain small towns like Malton or Driffield in Yorkshire, as well as those of their more important rivals.[8] For all their undoubted significance, however, as parts of the connective fabric of past life, the various socio-economic links between country and town to which allusion has been made (and others) have yet to be fitted into a sociological perception of their full implications in a societal sense, and even for the late periods discussed, by when towns were unquestionably exercising a more dominant role than in previous periods. When rural marketing centres lay thicker on the ground in medieval times the spatial pattern was clearly different.[9] It would certainly be simplistic as well as premature to subsume all rural communities or their social areas at any period into economically defined hinterlands, and then to claim that the populations concerned comprised, in some way, broadly recognizable social entities – not least when towns lay at the meeting points of contrasting agricultural regions.

The same may be said of regions in general. Regions may, of course, be defined in a number of ways, but a definition reached according to one scale of reference should not be transmuted automatically into another. Urban regions, agricultural regions, and administrative regions very rarely coincide precisely: the regional historian who does not take steps beyond that of acknowledging this basic fact is likely in some sense to be distorting his findings inadvertently as a result of squeezing them into a single mould. In the context of the present quest for definable arenas of social relations wider than the single community, yet narrower than that of the national society, therefore, it must be clear that 'regions' which are not *socially* defined – and they never are – cannot usefully be pressed into service to fill that gap.

In this search, the one remaining alternative is the society of the *pays*. Even here there are problems. Not all countrysides of a similar type necessarily followed the parallel lines of social development by which they are said usually to have been characterized. For example, despite an underlying matrix of similarity to other 'forest' areas, the woodland district of Shropshire (where, in at least one settlement, manorialism was not all that weak) singularly failed to experience the to-be-expected problems of over-population and massive poverty. Woodland by-employments did not proliferate; lawlessness was not a characteristic of the region; and nonconformity failed to put down early vigorous roots.[10]

Nor were *pays* homogeneous within themselves. In many regions of England their very delimitation indeed poses considerable problems, given the bewildering frequency with which soil patterns change. At a detailed level, allowance must always be made, therefore, for transitional zones between *pays* – fen-edge parishes and woodland-edge settlements, for example – which share more than one topographic characteristic. Even the inner settlements within a *pays* may vary markedly in terms of their manorial structures, the sizes of their parishes, and not least, in their differing susceptibilities to change and transformation. It is important not to exaggerate the number of exceptions to the general rule, but a note of caution has to be struck when seeking to characterize single communities in terms of the *pays* in which they are situated. As classificatory sub-types are ingeniously proliferated, the precise nature of the links between each community and the 'genius' of its countryside will become ever more difficult to establish. As the years pass, especially during the seventeenth and eighteenth centuries, increasing numbers of parishes will be 'taken out' of their traditional settings, and their identifying characteristics will be often altered beyond recognition, especially where 'open' becomes 'closed', in the landholding sense of those terms.[11] For all these reasons, it might seem premature to assume that, if they were recoverable, the 'social areas' of variously developed communities within any one *pays* would be sufficiently interlocking and spatially biased as to allow us to speak of them collectively as, for instance, a 'woodland society' coterminous with an entire countryside. The fact remains that in societal terms no *pays* as a whole has yet been defined in detail on the ground and then analysed in similar detail with respect to all its component 'communities' (exceptions included) and to the overall social characteristics and social inter-relationships that collectively they might have been expected to exhibit. In addition, we know very little yet about the relations between the societies of neighbouring *pays*. Once again, perhaps, not only should we return to the problems posed by the attractive rival powers of those market centres which, in this case, mediated *between* two or more *pays*, but we need also to remind ourselves of the strong evidence which survives for inter-regional migration patterns.

If at present, therefore, the quest for some sociologically significant, socio-spatial reality 'higher' than that of the local community does not seem entirely hopeless, the prospects hardly appear encouraging. The 'units' of investigation conventionally adopted by local historians often *seem* to be societal in their character and potentially societal in a wider sense, yet, with but a few exceptions, they have been analysed mainly with a view to the establishment of socio-economic rather than social structural processes.

Is there then a moral that might be drawn from this necessarily brief survey? It is, it may be suggested, that local and even generalist historians of society are not yet posing the same questions as sociologists or, perhaps more correctly, since we are discussing small-scale societies, as anthropologists. The divergence flows inevitably not from differences of interest, but also from what initially determines the units of study chosen. The historian now usually selects his local community or society (and frequently with some particular socio-economic historical problem already in mind), on the basis of two alternative criteria: either the availability of rich documentation that is the product of a given administrative entity like a manor, a borough or a county; or, in wider terms, in the context of a relatively homogeneous geographical locality – a *pays* or the 'Lake counties' for example – which is more or less readily identifiable. The anthropologist, by contrast, normally chooses a previously known *society*, and in that context then locates some spatially definable area within its territory for detailed investigation. For the one a territory is first defined and a 'society' then 'discovered' and studied with it; for the other a society is already identified, and only then is a sample of its territory deliberately selected. The two operations are quite different. Conversely, and as a result, the historian may find himself trapped in an illogical circular argument. Having defined a territory and then having discovered a community within it, the danger is that he will then relate the community once again to the territory. Yet 'community' belongs to a societal scale of reference while territory, be it a township area, a *pays* or a 'region', does not. Conceptually, 'community' as a social entity relates not to a geographic or to a socio-economic context, influential as those contexts may be on many major characteristics of a community; 'community' relates in the first place to the wider local society within which it is embedded.

If then in theory historians could identify ways of allowing regional or local societies as it were to 'define themselves' on the ground *before* they sample the constituent 'communities' within such 'societies', they might at least escape those criticisms of determinism that may so easily be levied against the nature of their prior-selection procedures. More than that, such an approach should help to illuminate both the nature of those socio-spatial orders that are wider than that of the single community and also the links between these different levels.

In seeking to translate aspiration into practice we may at least begin in the certain knowledge that such societies, to whatever degree they may have interlocked with their neighbours, did undoubtedly exist. The testimony of our own ears and personal experiences alone should persuade us that regional societies still survive to this day, and we need go back no more than a hundred years to discover how much stronger then was local identification with these societies. Difficult as it will be to identify and to dissect such societies, and then to connect them with the wider society of the nation, it is the central contention of this essay that the time has now come in the development of English local history as a subject for prime consideration to be given to this crucial element in our understanding of the English past. That of course is not to say that the scope of the subject now should be narrowed to include only such investigations, nor is it to claim that studies into rural and urban communities, into *pays* or into regions, let alone analyses of historic landscapes, are in any way outmoded. Most of England remains unexplored in all these respects and each fresh and ever more systematic approach to a yet unstudied area acts as a fundamental check on, and a corrective to, the probable biases – especially the inevitable documentary biases – inherent in studies made elsewhere. Yet if English local history is to concern itself more deeply, as it is beginning to do already, with societal as opposed to more socio-economic matters, the framework of analysis will need to be both adjusted and widened. It is then to one possible way in which this might be attempted that we must now turn, and in the light, be it emphasized, of much hitherto uncoordinated thinking that has marked the recent work not only of generalist historians, but also more especially of those concentrating on localized subjects.

Chapter 4

A Possible Societal Framework

We begin our public affections in our families . . . We pass on to our
neighbourhood, and our habitual provincial connections. These are inns and resting-
places. Such divisions of our country as have been formed by habit, and not by a
sudden jerk of authority, were so many little images of the great country in which
the heart found something which it could fill.

(Edmund Burke, *Reflections on the Revolution in France*, ed. Conor Cruise O'Brien,
(1969, p. 315)

A starting point might be to pursue the logic of the fact that a society is more
than a collectivity of people living within some shared structure; it is too a
ceaseless process not only at the level of social inter-relationships but also in
terms of its membership. Where physical mobility is highly localized the
memberships of particular communities may be constantly changing, but over
the same area as a whole there may well emerge comparatively dense networks
of blood relationships, the perpetuation of which in one form or another over
generations will be likely to engender traditionalized modes of local self-
identification and hence, in cultural terms, some sense of local exclusiveness. In
a largely oral culture, for example, this may be most obviously expressed in
terms of local dialect, but other customary and similarly demarcatory characteristics will be equally important. The first question that needs to be asked,
therefore, is whether historical evidence survives for the bunching of English
people into the same generally definable territories as those in which they were
born and, if so, what appears to have been the average maximal spatial
constraint on the movement of the majority?

The earliest dates for which a national picture may be obtained are those of the
mid-nineteenth-century censuses from which a broad county by county
panorama emerges. The evidence is certainly not perfect. There may well have
been some confusion as to whether 'county' meant ancient county or, more
properly, Registration county – a difficult matter when ancient boundaries were
frequently overlapped by registration districts – but the results of these enquiries
were nevertheless remarkable. Even after a period of rapidly rising population
and massive urbanization, it could be reported in 1851, for example, that 'of
17,165,656 persons born in England and Wales, 13,691,914, or 80 per cent, were
enumerated in the [Registration] county of their birth.'[1] When allowances are
made for the fact that this proportion is heavily weighted by children too young
to have moved on their own accounts, the total is still significant. Arbitrarily
taking 14 as the age by which most children would have been leaving home, the
percentage of children at or under that age only represented 36 per cent of the
total population in 1851.[2] An overwhelming majority of adult residents in most
shires, therefore, must have been county-born; others may have been about to

return to their native heaths from temporary residence elsewhere.

A national proportion of 80 per cent, of course, disguises a considerable degree of regional variation which also should be understood over a longer timescale. By 1851 the erosion of the indigenous English provinces was already under way, as a comparison between the relative standings of the shires in this respect for both 1841 and 1861 makes plain. The shift that is so vividly illustrated below (despite some technical difficulties in comparing the figures available for both these years), is sufficient at least to indicate that the patterns which obtained in 1841 are hardly likely to misrepresent to any serious degree, the probable state of affairs that had traditionally existed in the preceding period.[3]

Numbers of English counties in descending categories by percentages of inhabitants born within each county: 1841 and 1861

% County born	Numbers of counties	
	1841	1861
90–94.9	7[a]	2
85–89.9	10[b]	4[c]
80–84.9	11	8
75–79.9	12	11
70–74.9	–	8
65–69.9	–	4
60–64.9	2	1
55–59.9	1	1
50–54.9	–	1
Total counties	43	40

a   Including 3 divisions of Yorkshire
b   Including 1 division of Yorkshire
c   Including the whole of Yorkshire

The general reduction in the proportion of native inhabitants by county across the country between 1841 and 1861 may hardly be denied from these figures overall. In 1841, when the four parts of Yorkshire (including York City and Ansty) are combined to count as one county, 37 out of 40 shires could boast over three-quarters of their enumerated populations as native. In 1861, only 25 counties out of 40 could claim the same. In each of these years, the lowest percentages recorded were those for Monmouthshire, Middlesex and Surrey respectively and in that descending order. Even in 1861, however, 37 out of 40 counties still contained a proportion of over 65 per cent locally born inhabitants: from County Durham with 67.58 per cent to Cornwall with 91.94 per cent.

The picture that emerges for 1841, therefore, is particularly significant. The most conservative areas are much as might have been expected if we take as our cut-off point a minimum base-line of 85 per cent natives as opposed to 75 per cent per county concerned. On this basis certain wider regions stand out as well as a number of exceptional single counties. Thus the area of the West Country and much of Hardy's Wessex together (but excluding Hampshire which, incidentally, experienced the heaviest drop in its native population between

1841 and 1861: from 82.8 per cent down to 71.01 per cent), emerges as divided into the most indigenously populated counties: Cornwall (the national leader with 94.8 per cent), Devon (90.4), Dorset (89.1), Wiltshire (88.3) and Somerset (86.7). The same was true of East Anglia with Essex – Norfolk (93.2 per cent), Suffolk (91.3) and Essex (86.3); and of much of the rest of Eastern England: the four divisions of Yorkshire which ranged from native proportions of 89.3 in the East Riding to 92.3 in the North and West Ridings; and Lincolnshire with a proportion of 89.9 per cent. The remaining counties at this level, however, stand out in a more isolated fashion: Cumberland with 86.3 per cent was bordered by Westmorland with 79.8 per cent; Sussex with 85.2 per cent was to be contrasted to Kent with only 77.9; while Shropshire's proportion of 85.2 per cent (closely shadowed by Herefordshire to the south with 84.0) was nevertheless neighboured to the north by Cheshire with but 75.9 per cent. In the Midlands only Leicestershire (85.3 per cent) lay above the mark, but it was closely followed below that line by Northamptonshire, Derbyshire, Bedfordshire and Cambridgeshire in that order.

The recitation of such figures is tedious, but at this, the most unambiguous level of the table, where by definition the counties concerned have suffered least from the diluting effects of recent immigration, two major points may be said to flow inexorably from them. First, and outside the major areas of urbanization and industrialization (which in many cases anyway distort the proportions of natives still resident in county countrysides), the most conservative areas of the country lay either towards a seaboard and/or towards a 'national' inland boundary between England and Scotland or Wales. As was to be expected, such regions lay at the peripheries of the country on either natural or cultural frontiers across which immigration for whatever purpose – marriage or economic betterment, for example – would have been less than usually common. Which said, it has to be stressed also that nearly a third of all the 40 counties of England, and a substantial proportion of its land-mass, is thus embraced in this upper echelon of indigenously biased county populations.

A second point may also be demonstrated in this connection. If now, simply for the sake of argument, we restrict our observations to the top ten counties on the table (including the four divisions of Yorkshire), all of which boasted proportions of native residents in excess of 89 per cent, then the relative immobility over one generation of some *neighbouring* county populations is most striking. In the western peninsula, while barely more than five per cent of Cornwall's inhabitants were immigrants, it nonetheless remains a matter for remark that in excess of 90 per cent of Devon's resident population in 1841 had been born there. We may perhaps allow that a major topographical obstacle, like the river Humber, might have partly accounted for the respective and heavily introverted population stocks of Yorkshire and Lincolnshire, but what then are we also to make of the manifest lack of demographic integration not only between Devon and Cornwall, Dorset and Somerset, but also between such shires as Norfolk and Suffolk in both of which last the county natives accounted for over 91 per cent of their respective resident populations? In this latter case, at least, physical restrictions on mobility between these two eastern shires other than, or even including, the gentle valley of the river Waveney, were minimal. Something else clearly constrained movement between the two counties, and while it may yet prove that a southward pull drew more people from Norfolk into Suffolk than vice versa, the fact remains that the major obstacle to movement between the two shires appears to have been the invisible frontier between them. In both cases, fewer than nine per cent of their resident populations represented immigrants from *anywhere* outside their own boundaries in 1841.

Peripheral cases, it might be argued, make for extreme illustrations especially where the data is presented in a highly generalized way. As a counterpoint let us then turn in detail to the instance of a land-locked, inland county that at this date was sufficiently removed from the immediate pull of the capital, but which lay well outside the remoter regions of the Highland Zone. Bedfordshire was neither culturally remote like Dorset nor, because of the undramatic south-east midland landscape within which it lies, was it inaccessible to population movements. Mainly agrarian in its own pursuits, surrounded by equally agricultural counties, and thus largely innocent of those trends towards urbanization and heavy industrialization that together conspired to undermine what appear at first sight to have been the former patterns of localized longevity of residence, Bedfordshire perhaps may be taken here as a tentative indication of residential patterns even before 1841.[4]

The distribution of Bedfordshire's native inhabitants is instructive (see fig. 1). Even in the 53 parishes which border on other counties the average proportion of Bedfordshire natives was 78.8 per cent, a remarkably high figure even when allowance is made for children, while in ten of these parishes the proportion of outsiders did not exceed 14 per cent. Within this frontier zone, as it were, the average proportion of native inhabitants of all the 76 parishes which comprise the 'interior', reached as high as 89.3 per cent of the total populations concerned. A generalized 'contour' map of parish densities, indeed, shows that over a wide area extending to within one parish short of the county boundary in the west, and to within one, two or three parishes short of the boundary elsewhere, 90 per cent or more of the inhabitants of each parish were county natives. In a continuously narrow, off-central, swathe of territory, one parish in breadth, and running from south-west to north-east (and in four isolated parochial outliers), the proportion rises to over 95 per cent, the highest figure recorded being 98 per cent for the parish of Pulloxhill which lies a mere three miles or so from the county boundary.

Many more such studies need to be made, and over wider regions than this, before we may conclude that the county always comprised a crucial but invisible territorial constraint on local mobility. Yet in the national context already discussed, the Bedfordshire pattern emerges as no more than might have been expected. If the county did act in such a generalized way, outside the towns the edges of it obviously would have tended to comprise the areas most susceptible to immigration, while some sort of rural native core also might have been predicated. (In other counties, where the leading town was centrally placed, more than one such core perhaps might be expected.)

That the English shires may have long performed a similar containing function is also suggested by earlier evidence. In a study of 2,268 individuals from the townships in the Plain of York between 1777 and 1822, for example, Dr B. A. Holderness has been able to show that only 18 per cent migrated more than ten

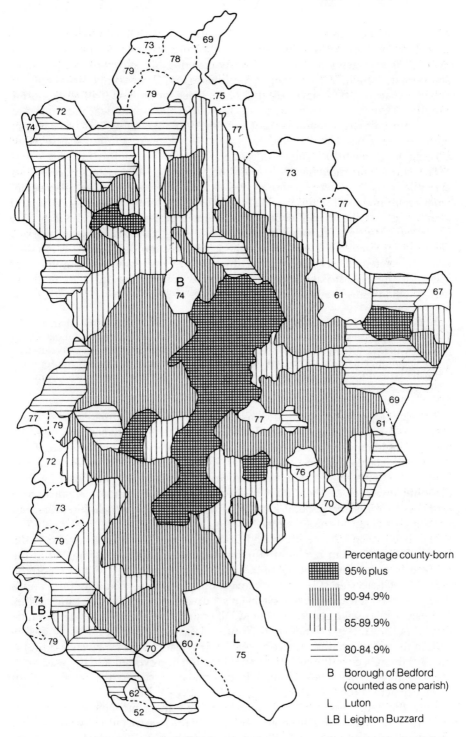

Figure 1 Bedfordshire in 1841 (1834 boundaries): percentage densities of native inhabitants by parochial areas (based on information provided by Mr Peter Gray)

miles, and that of this minority, in excess of four in every five had moved within Yorkshire itself.[5] For the period 1660–1730, Professor Peter Clark's analysis of over 7,000 deponents at diocesan courts covering all or parts of 11 counties, shows that overall, 77.0 per cent of rural males and 79 per cent of rural females either remained 'stationary' in the same place or moved within the same county.[6] It can have been no accident, then, that the county was recognized as the appropriate administrative unit for the Marriage Act of 1653, compliance with which, it has been argued recently, was possible simply because of an existing 'strict regard for the county boundary'.[7]

   The short-scale movements in question, however, all relate to lifetime or life-cycle mobility whereas, and as was argued at the start of this discussion, what really matters for the establishment of some form of social and cultural identity, is the perpetuation of such confined patterns in broad areas over generations. In these circumstances we must turn to the accumulated work of *The English Surnames Survey* which, under the direction of Mr R. A. McKinley, has now systematically investigated this form of evidence over a number of counties. The most striking lesson to be derived from this careful study of nearly half a million individuals is that:

> In most English counties, the surnames present up to the 19th century retain a distinctively local character. . . In most areas of England, there is a substantial stock of surnames, which appear in each area when hereditary surnames first develop in sizeable numbers (often during the 13th and 14th centuries), and which still form the greater part of the local body of names at the start of the 19th century, and in many cases even later.[8]

Most tellingly, it is becoming increasingly probable that in the cases of those surnames which originated in local place-names, such locative names often go back to single families associated with identifiable farms or tiny hamlets. Even during industrialization in Lancashire or Yorkshire's West Riding, for example, later descendants of such families, all bearing the same surname (but by then probably unaware of their inter-relationship), may be traced in substantial numbers in the same general locality as that from which their forebears had sprung four centuries or so earlier.[9]

   The mechanism may be illustrated from one case. The main local line of the Leicestershire yeoman family of Humberstone seems to have originated in the thirteenth century in the village of that name just outside, and to the east of, the borough of Leicester. The family moved into the town, made its pile, and a junior branch then appears to have been set up in the neighbouring countryside. Thereafter successive generations gradually moved northwards to within a mile or two of the county boundary, then turned eastwards and eventually descri-bed, in their slow migration, a complete circle which, in the nineteenth century, brought them back to the county town where the line expired. On the way, they seem to have taken Leicestershire brides; never once did the family set up residence across the boundary.[10]

   Now the Humberstones may have confined their movements to Leices-tershire, but what is equally noticeable is that they restricted themselves even more particularly: to what roughly may be described as the north-east quadrant of the county and thus very largely to the broad arc of the Leicestershire wolds –

a distinctive *pays*. Each move involved a small-scale step and in this they may have been not untypical of many families at a broadly similar level of landholding in the same shire. W. G. Hoskins, for example, was also able to trace the fluctuating propensity to movement of some dozen or so yeoman families over the centuries and also within relatively constricted areas. He was even able to conclude (but from his wider knowledge in general) that the majority of the rural population 'did not move far, perhaps as far as Leicester, but more often only a parish or two away . . . Their names remained rooted in the same small district, within a radius of half a dozen miles or less.'[11] This was markedly true of certain farming families studied by Dr Cicely Howell in the champion area around Kibworth Harcourt in the same county during the fourteenth and fifteenth centuries in particular. Land in a half dozen parishes or so in the immediate vicinity, it would seem, was 'temporarily' occupied, and sometimes re-occupied, by certain families even within comparatively short periods; while five of these parishes had enough in common in 1414 to furnish an isolated sprinkling of supporters in the Lollard cause.[12] It seems to have been equally true of a number of family dynasties which circulated through another bloc of five or six parishes near Kimcote and Gilmorton at the southern end of Leicestershire from the fifteenth or sixteenth centuries onwards.[13] Leicestershire yeomen frequently held freehold land in adjacent parishes simultaneously; so too in the Warwickshire 'felden', where the freehold family of Mann, for example, had first appeared at Harbury in 1569 or before. According to Dr J. K. Martin, 'In the eighteenth century nine families of this name received allotments under the [enclosure] awards of five neighbouring parishes.'[14] The most systematic work on this subject, however, is that done by Professor Alan Everitt on nineteenth-century Kent – a region not of common fields, but of ancient enclosure. There, on the basis of 1,143 farming families in his sample (44 per cent of whom were mainly small freeholders), he was able to trace 'some 221 "paramount" dynasties' which 'comprised 4,450 separately established branches altogether virtually all of which were confined to Kent', whether these branches were still in farming or not. Above all, such families were usually restricted to limited parochial neighbourhoods, the extreme case being the 57 branches of the Collard family, no fewer than 44 of which lived 'in a group of neighbouring parishes around St Nicholas-at-Wade, between Canterbury and Thanet'.[15]

It was dynasties like these, of course, that for long comprised the typical and usually small semi-permanent cores of so many rural communities. Not that they always had to be freehold farmers, however. Security of tenure, and hence longevity of family residence, could also be assured in some areas, as in Shropshire from the sixteenth to the later eighteenth century, once copyholds had been replaced by three-life leases.[16] Nor did such families have to be tied to the land: increasingly perhaps as the eighteenth century progressed, rural community-cores may have tended to include occupational lineages like the boat-people of Oxford or the blacksmiths of Kent, many of whom may be proved to have been of ancient Kentish stock.[17] In towns, Professor Everitt has underlined the growing importance since the seventeenth century of a wide range of occupational lineages.[18]

To some implications of such patterns it will be necessary to revert. Before doing so, however, it must be stressed that so far this discussion has built downwards, as it were, in an inevitably cursory fashion from the county, to the neighbourhood, to the community core, and with increasing emphasis on the semi-permanence of some family lines. It is clearly not enough to concentrate on dynasties alone (though it is relevant to note that the locations of such dynastic patterns on the ground, would have been in their turn the outcome of initial short-term moves); what also matters is the degree to which the majority of the population eddied and flowed over time around, and in connection with, such 'stable' families. The rate of turnover within particular communities, after all, was clearly extraordinarily high. If, to recall but two examples, on average 'only one family in ten in the Leicestershire village of 1525 had been settled in the same place for five generations'; Peter Laslett's more detailed information for whole households from seventeenth-century Clayworth, Nottinghamshire, and Cogenhoe in Northamptonshire, has demonstrated that in the former place no fewer than 60.8 per cent of all the inhabitants in 1676 left or died within a mere 12 years, and in the latter, 52 per cent of the population of 1618 vanished within ten.[19] The population in general was highly mobile both in medieval and later times, though there are hints that there may have been periods – before the Black Death, or the late seventeenth century – when it was rather less mobile than in others.[20] Whichever the case, it is clear enough that physical mobility was very largely short-range in character.

The mechanisms of localized mobility are broadly understood. In early modern England, at the latest, adolescents sent out to service or to take up apprenticeships travelled comparatively short distances, and in those cases where employment was taken up thereafter on an annual basis, the yearly moves were also within relatively restricted areas: the tendency for hiring fairs in pastoral regions to be held in early summer, and for those in arable regions to be held in the autumn alone making it difficult for a farm servant easily to transfer from one *pays* to another.[21] Even before the age of hiring fairs, moreover, it is evident enough that villeins, for example, tended to move within narrow districts: of the 126 serfs withdrawing from the Norfolk manor of Forncett, between 1400 and 1575, over 70 per cent settled at places within about 12 miles of it (including Norwich).[22] Marriages, moreover, usually took place between partners who appear to have resided within five, ten or a dozen miles of each other not only in the age of parish registers whence such figures are calculable, but also probably long before. In the Anglo-Saxon period, it seems to have been assumed that the kindreds involved in betrothal agreements, for example, would usually have been resident on the estate of the same thegn, while possibly the earliest fragmentary evidence for marriage horizons, from eleventh-century Hertfordshire, implies again a range of up to 12 miles between the partners.[23] At any period, perhaps, even if young couples moved after their weddings, only some people setting up home can have done so at vast distances from their places of birth. Because of this limited 'circular mobility' as Peter Clark has aptly termed it,[24] the immediate social frame of reference was intensely localized. Long distance migration concerned only a minority: short distance migration was as likely as not to have been to some neighbouring locality or town.

Of the mechanisms involved in short-range mobility, it is clear that for present purposes spatial patterns of marriage are the most relevant since marriages create identifiable webs of new social relationships over definable districts. For all its drawbacks, therefore, the evidence for marriage-horizons represents the nearest we are likely to get in creating a basis for societal analysis across entire regions from the mid-eighteenth century onwards, and for many parts of such regions in preceding periods too: as always historians must make do with imperfect materials. If, moreover, we were to embark on such a regional analysis and thus seek to escape from the methodological confines of the single community-focused study, we might also in part overcome one of the major difficulties associated with the understanding of such marriage horizons: the spatial relationship between the places mentioned as the 'residences' of the partners concerned (and of the brides especially) and the places where the couples actually settled.[25] The study of areas wider than that of the single parish should help to reduce the risk that conclusions are being very seriously skewed by such considerations. Albeit in a generalized way, it should prove possible eventually to demarcate, at least for later periods, broad areas within counties (or overlapping county boundaries) which were marked either by a strong propensity towards in-marriage or a tendency to marry out. In particular, it will thus be necessary that attention be paid in any exercise of this kind to the relative densities of reciprocation between parishes or between individual settlements *within* such a district.

These aspirations depend on rather more than pious hopes. There are already a number of studies which, although usually based on single settlements, indicate a variety of common factors that served to bias marriage horizons in some directions rather than others. They may be swiftly summarized. First, where population is relatively dense, partners will be more readily available in the immediate neighbourhood: more in-marriage may therefore be expected within some *pays* (as opposed to individual rural communities) than in others.[26] An ingenious study of marriage-licences in early seventeenth-century Kent, for example, shows that the large well-populated wealden parishes, which contained numerous dispersed settlements, were likely to be more endogamous than the small under-populated parishes of the wolds.[27] In other areas, like the unhealthy Essex marshes, it may have been neccessary for the menfolk from families that had become relatively immune to the marsh ague to import their brides from the nearby uplands.[28] Second, within *pays*, it is clear that even quite minor geographical features tended to prejudice or even channel the contacts involved. Watersheds or ridges manifestly separated the inhabitants of settlements in adjacent parishes in, for example, Northamptonshire, Huntingdonshire or Dorset.[29] Third, major geographical obstacles obviously restricted choice even further: a chain of hills, a navigable river, or the sea might each limit the area of selection by up to 180 degrees or more.[30] Fourth, there is the attractive power of towns and hence the communications through the countryside to them. In these cases, courtship patterns clearly tended to funnel from wayside settlements, or from occupational communities involved in water-borne activities, along the axes of either the road or navigable river concerned.[31] For rural females dwelling in urban vicinities, in particular perhaps, the attraction of towns over adjacent countrysides was probably stronger still.[32] A final consideration, and one of the highest significance for the understanding of shire 'societies', is that in certain areas but not in others, work is beginning to show that the county boundary itself may have proved some sort of cultural as opposed to physical obstacle to marriage across it. Inter-marriage across the boundary between Huntingdonshire and Cambridgeshire in the later seventeenth century thus appears to have been minimal; while the frontier between southern Nottinghamshire and Derbyshire in the same century posed no such barrier.[33]

What then are the general implications of this discussion for the central problem of this paper? First it may be argued that rural communities can only be understood as parts of a spatial and 'processual' continuum. In the long term, communities are, as it were, no more than staging posts, through which some families pass briefly and others move more slowly. Secondly, the combination of inter-parochial marriage patterns, 'dynastic' neighbourhoods and the supra-parochial distributions of landholding or of localized craft specialisms, should allow the prior identification of the social or kinship localities within which the communities that are internal to them may then be studied. Many such localities away from towns will probably broadly coincide with, or, where there are either geographical barriers or major lines of communication cutting through them, will be socially 'separated' parts of, identifiable *pays*. Finally, where such localities do not reflect continuous stretches of homogeneous countryside, they will be unlikely to overlap shire boundaries.

Two final suggestions flow from these matters and will bear closer subsequent discussion. On the one hand, it may be proposed that some shire societies will prove to have had 'edges' at certain points (as may well have been the case in eastern Bedfordshire in 1841 – see fig. 1), as opposed to a somewhat diluted, intermixed buffer zone adjacent to a neigbouring county (as seems to have been true of western Bedfordshire in 1841). Such latter areas of 'overlap' may be especially conspicuous where continuous stretches of homogeneous coun-tryside, like the wealden region of Sussex and Kent, cut across the county divisions. Similarly, where substantial towns in neighbouring counties are closely linked by busy communication routes across their borders, such 'edges' are hardly to be expected. Where shire and/or ancient diocesan boundaries coincide with geographical obstacles, however, the existence of cultural barriers will also be likely: the 'beck'/'burn' division of the names for watercourses between the ancient counties of Cumberland and Northumberland or Durham, that is broadly defined on the map not only by the Pennines but also by shire and diocesan boundaries, is an obvious example.[34] Within counties, and away from such 'edges', it is improbable that social localities or neighbourhoods will be so clearly demarcated except where pronounced internal geographical features obtrude, as in the case perhaps of the Dartmoor barrier between east and west in southern Devon.

On the other hand, where definable 'edges' exist – and be they physically or culturally delimited – it would seem to follow that since the potential field for the choice of marriage partners may be 'halved' thereby, the social localities or the communities within them will tend to be more tight-knit in kinship terms than those elsewhere and, when that is the case, demarcatory cultural traits will be correspondingly strong. It is possible to furnish examples from both physical and cultural frontiers.

The implications of physical barriers in this respect need only be dealt with briefly. One instance in question might be the society inhabiting the vast parish of

Shap in Cumbria (earlier northern Westmorland), the territory of which runs up to one of the few passes permitting egress southwards to Kendal and Lancashire. Marked by an appallingly bad road until the mid-eighteenth century (and a not much better one until the days of the M6), Shap parish stretched largely over tracts of uninviting fells – westward to Mardale – and southwards, over both fells and the pass, towards Kendal. (It may be added, incidentally, that at that point, the parish boundary coincided not only with the southern boundary of Carlisle diocese, and of the early twelfth-century *potestas* of Carlisle, but also with that of the Barony of Appleby which, only in the thirteenth century, was finally combined with the Barony of Kendal to create that most artificial of ancient county units, Westmorland.[35] In Shap parish parochial endogamy rates reached the excessively high levels of 71 per cent for males and 94 per cent for females (though, of course, some of these females may have returned from elsewhere in order to be married). Especially significant, therefore, is the remarkable persistence of surnames in the parish through from the sixteenth and early seventeenth centuries to the end of the eighteenth. Higher than normal kinship densities must be inferred from the fact that 'About one-sixth of the names found in the last quarter of the eighteenth century are also found continuously in periods stretching back to the last quarter of the sixteenth century.'[36] More extreme still may be the case of the topographically isolated fishing village of Robin Hood's Bay in Yorkshire where, despite marriages outwards both northwards and southwards along the east coast, 13 family names present in 1540 were still being held by no fewer than 130 people in 1841 when two of these surnames alone were being shared by 90 people. Taking the 'surrounding' parish of Fylingdales as a whole, 27 surnames once connected, or still connected, with Robin Hood's Bay, survived from 1540 and were borne by 193 persons in 1841. In all, some 41.6 per cent of the enumerated population of the village alone in 1841 bore surnames that had entered the parish by 1650.[37]

Cultural barriers, too, clearly conspired to influence the nature of their adjacent societies, and nowhere would this have been more marked than along national frontiers. The Anglo-Scottish frontier was in a sense a product of both physical and cultural factors. Sour soils, hills and the barely controlled no-man's land that straddled the political boundary all conspired to create that distinctive feuding society of the 'Surnames' which flourished on a diet of 'blackmail' and ballads in the area between the fourteenth and the seventeenth centuries.[38] It may not be irrelevant to note, moreover, that south of this national boundary the mapping of blood groups in Northumberland today still shows a genetic divide between two separate groups, the one on Tyneside and the other occupying the less hospitable upland regions running up to the Scottish border.[39] Similarly, it has also been shown that the earlier Herefordshire boundary between England and Wales, also separates two blood groups.[40] In neither border region does much inter-marriage between the different populations thus seem to be implied.

The probable influence of cultural constraints on a local population, however, is perhaps more instructively testable in the centre of the gentle undulating felden areas of the Midland plain, by looking at two points on the common boundary between Leicestershire and Warwickshire at two different periods (fig.2). For this boundary can hardly be regarded as coinciding with an insuperable physical barrier preventing movement between the two counties: it broadly shadows the central Midlands watershed which lies marginally to its west, but the contouring is very gradual, and across it the distances between settlements are not great.

In studying this boundary zone, therefore, the cultural factor cannot be ignored. For this was a frontier of immense antiquity. As I have argued elsewhere,[41] for at least some of its length, the boundary may have broadly corresponded formerly to a prehistoric division of peoples and then later to a Roman recognition of that fact: the Roman Watling Street roughly defines most of the boundary's length. In the Anglo-Saxon period we are on slightly safer ground: at this point, it was almost certainly the boundary between the Mercians and those Middle Angles who inhabited the Leicestershire area, while later still, probably in the tenth century, it was definitely the south-western edge of the Viking territory of the Five Boroughs, one of which was Leicester. It was a diocesan boundary and, probably from some point in the eleventh century, it became the county boundary.[42] By, or during, the eighteenth century it came to constitute an economic boundary: the outwork villages of the silk ribbon-weaving industry centred on Coventry stretched up to the more northerly end of the Warwickshire side of the border; and the hosiery industry centred on Leicester or Hinckley spread out to the Leicestershire side.[43] Such overlap as there was seems to have been minimal. Finally, Watling Street appears to represent one of those few significant dialect boundaries that cautious modern experts are now prepared to recognize.[44]

Now north of the point where the Leicestershire boundary departs from the Watling Street, and thus at the western end of the shire, lies the dual settlement of Appleby Magna and Appleby Parva. Over the Warwickshire border, some two miles away from the latter, is one of two equally close Warwickshire settlements, the village of Austrey, whose parish boundary abuts that of Appleby. Both Austrey and Appleby have recently been subjected to micro-scopic investigation (including family reconstitution) by Dr Alan Roberts, for the later sixteenth and the seventeenth centuries; and his results seem to corroborate the arguments already presented. For marriage partners, for hirings, for markets, for debt involvements, the inhabitants of these two neighbouring 'frontier' parishes very largely looked in quite opposite directions, and in both cases towards their respective parent county-territories. More than this, by comparison with Keith Wrightson's Terling in mid-Essex, kinship densities were extraordinarily high. At Terling a mere 39.3 per cent of the 122 householders and their affines in 1671 were found to be inter-related (this being a minimal calculation). By contrast, at Austrey minimum kinship densities reached 80 per cent (out of 84 taxable households in 1670), and at Appleby (1663–70), the proportion rose to 86 per cent of the 91 taxable households concerned.[45]

It might be argued here, perhaps, that given the growing contemporary influence of the 'local market area', it was this factor above all others that may have determined these marked patterns. Austrey lay at an almost identical distance from its nearest market centre, Tamworth (and indeed from Ather-stone), as Appleby lay from Ashby-de-la-Zouch (about five miles). Both par-ishes, it might be thought, were thus situated at the outer peripheries of their respective market areas. Comparison with the contemporary behaviour of other rural settlements which were comparably situated *vis-à-vis* their local market

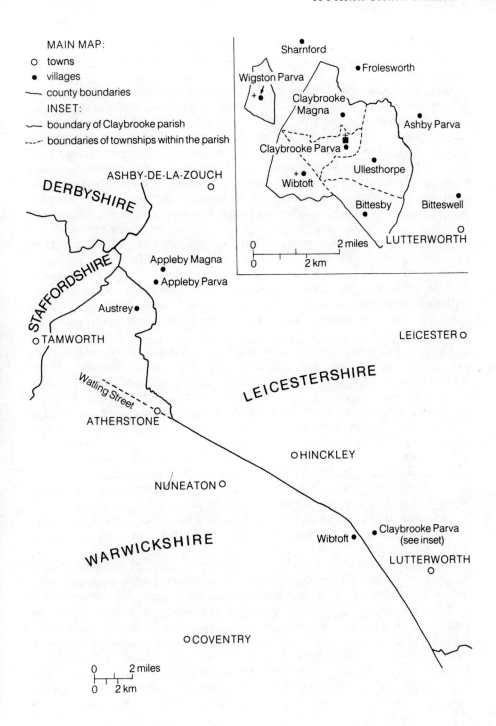

Figure 2   Leicestershire and Warwickshire settlements discussed in the text

centres, however, hardly helps to confirm this hypothesis. Contacts with different towns up to five, seven, even nine miles away, appear to have been commonplace.[46]

The possible complication of the rival urban hinterland in relation to this county division, however, may be confidently eliminated when we turn to an area approximately half-way along the Watling Street line where in earlier times it had been crossed by the Fosse Way. The centre of the abnormally extensive parish of Claybrooke, with its seven settlements of varying size set in some 5,300 acres all told, lay more or less equidistant between, and five or six miles apart from, two Leicestershire towns: the market town of Lutterworth to the south-east, and the framework knitting centre of Hinckley to the north-west. During the seventeenth century, Claybrooke parish has been convincingly shown to have lain agriculturally on, or even across, the outer perimeter of the market area of Lutterworth.[47] Framework knitting, by contrast, which had been introduced in or by the early eighteenth century, was then connected north-westwards to Hinckley, but whether that connection survived is not known.[48] By 1846, perhaps significantly, total weekly carrier connections between three settlements in the parish and nearby towns on market days numbered five with Hinckley, four with Leicester, and only two with Lutterworth and Coventry (in Warwickshire).[49]

All six of the Leicestershire 'communities' connected with the parish were situated less than a mile and a half to the east of the county boundary: of the 1,438 persons concerned, 82.5 per cent were county-born in 1841.[50] The only community with less than 74 per cent such, was a 'deserted medieval village' comprising three houses (with 50 per cent); the highest scores were recorded in another wholly agricultural hamlet of nine households (a detached Leicestershire chapelry) in which no less than 94 per cent of the population was Leicestershire-born, and, close to it, in a largely Leicestershire wayside settlement actually on the Watling Street, where the proportion rose to 100 per cent.[51] At one further settlement, Wibtoft, another chapelry of the parish, which was situated almost beside the Watling Street but on its other, western, side in Warwickshire, there is a suspicion that there may have been some confusion as to what was meant by 'county', so the figure (74 per cent born ? in Leicestershire) is unfortunately difficult to interpret.

Between 1771 and 1841, a total of 439 marriage ceremonies was registered at the parish church in Claybrooke Parva. Of these 878 people, 91.1 per cent were said to have resided within five miles of the church; only 5.0 per cent from within five to ten miles; while a mere 3.9 per cent came from over ten miles. The parochial endogamy rate was 84.6 per cent, though the outsiders (overwhelmingly the grooms who presumably then 'removed' their brides) came from 76 parishes other than Claybrooke. A closer look at the origins of the 844 partners (including parishioners) from within the ten-mile limit, however, demonstrates that only 3.8 per cent of them came from the west of Watling Street when the chapelry at Wibtoft is counted as in Leicestershire. (If Wibtoft is counted as part of Warwickshire, the proportion from the west only rises to 6.2 per cent.)[52] More than this, of the seven nearest Warwickshire townships that embrace Claybrooke parish to the west, only four provided marriage partners for parishioners over this entire half-century (a mere 12 partners in 50 years). The closest

Warwickshire village, lying near to Watling Street and next to Wibtoft, provided none. Now what are essentially courtship-horizons, of course, do not necessarily indicate anything about the ultimate places of residence of new households, but one would need to be a cynic indeed to envisage a lemming-like post-marital rush of Leicestershire newly-weds across this sternly demarcated frontier. We are looking here, it seems to me, at the 'edge' of a shire 'society'. It is certainly relevant to note that by 1851, a mere 2 per cent of Leicestershire's entire population had been supplied from Warwickshire.[53]

On the Leicestershire side of the boundary (but including Wibtoft), moreover, there are some indications that four or five of the settlements concerned, together comprised an identifiable 'neighbourhood' which was but minimally connected even with adjacent parishes to the east. Of Claybrooke parish's seven immediate Leicestershire neighbours, three parishes furnished only one marriage partner each in 50 years; two provided three, and a further two proffered five and six partners respectively. There were connections beyond this line with the nearest Leicestershire market towns, especially Lutterworth, but again they were limited.[54] An analysis of kinship is thus able to concentrate on what might be called a well-defined core area.

The family reconstitution exercise on which the kinship results are based, however, was limited (because of earlier inadequacies in the parish register) to the period 1791–1841; the kinship connections are thus chronologically shallow to such an extent that, it may be confidently asserted, the interim figures to be cited represent absolute *minima*. On this basis, then, a familiar, and to be expected, picture soon emerges. Across the parish,[55] only 107 out of the 272 households in question (38.6 per cent) were linked by all forms of kinship *within* settlements – a figure that is not far removed from Keith Wrightson's minimum finding for Terling in 1671, where 39.3 per cent were so connected. The range of kinship links within these separate communities, however, was considerable: the percentages for the three smallest settlements (Wigston Parva, Claybrooke Parva and Wibtoft) were well below the overall proportion (22.2–17.4 per cent); while of the two largest settlements, Ullesthorpe's score fell only just below (35.7 per cent), yet that for Claybrooke Magna reached 52.6 per cent.[56] When connections *between* settlements are taken into account, moreover, the overall proportion of households connected rises to a minimal figure of 48.2 per cent. Had there been more generational depth in the family reconstitution exercise, the proportion would have been well in excess of 50 per cent. For the inter-household connections that may be effected for Claybrooke parish *in toto*, even on a 50-year basis, vastly exceed those established for Terling where it was not possible to identify relationships, between groups of more than four households. At Claybrooke, taken as a whole, practically 40 per cent of the households that may be so connected involve more than four households. There is one case each, involving links between six, seven, eight, 11 and, most remarkably of all, 20 households (17 of which were situated in one centre, Ullesthorpe).[57]

Insofar as we may therefore tell at present, we seem to have here a relatively self-contained kinship 'system' (highly concentrated on four of the settlements)[58] which – as the detailed figures show – was culturally 'bounded' to the south-west by the county boundary; which faded towards the north-west even within the parish; which, with the probable exception of certain farming families,[59] was not densely connected with neighbouring Leicestershire parishes to the east and south-east; and through which the rest of the population eddied and flowed. Of course there was inter-marriage with the outside world, and of course there was migration: the decadal imbalance between natural increase and the inter-censal increase is enough to demonstrate that; but considerable stability is also implied by the structure that may be reconstructed on the ground in 1841.

So brief a summary must inevitably be somewhat simplistic. Yet the outlines are reasonably firm. They suggest that it would be worth taking areas more extensive than single-settlement parishes elsewhere in the pursuit of such localized neighbourhoods, many of which may have extended over territories wider than this one. What is particularly suggestive in this case, however, is that the Claybrooke 'system' may perhaps illustrate not only the manner in which a neighbourhood identifies itself on the ground, but also the constraints imposed by, and the kinship densities that may result from, its location on the edge of a shire-society.

Chapter 5

Conclusion: Some Implications

It is perhaps somewhat qestionable if there be any department in literature in
which the writer has less to hope, or more to fear, than in that of local history. . .
To escape censure is therefore a privilege which no writer of provincial history has
any just reason to expect.

(Samuel Drew, ed., *The History of Cornwall from the Earliest Periods and Traditions to the
Present Time*, compiled by Fortescue Hitchins, 1824, I, p. iii)

This discussion has arisen out of two problems that appear to face English local
historians: how they may relate their detailed findings systematically to the
wider mosaic of English society as a past whole; and how, in doing so, they need
to discover ways in which to overcome at least some of the limitations posed by
many of their conventional objects of local inquiry. It is not suggested that the
solutions proposed here so crudely are the only solutions, nor that they will
necessarily prove to be entirely correct solutions. Huge areas of investigation
require to be filled before that can be known for certain and especially in the
context of reciprocal marriage patterns amongst groupings of communities over
entire districts; in the contexts of cultural 'boundaries' or frontier zones where
these may be broadly identified; and not least in the context of maps that reflect
those combinations of hereditary traits with which modern geneticists are
beginning to differentiate neighbouring sets of people today.[1] Nevertheless, it is
claimed that local historians need increasingly to face up to a potential *impasse* in
the definition of their subject, and that therefore it is useful to look at the field as
a whole from a fresh perspective which relies heavily on coordinating the
implications of a good deal of pioneering work that exists, albeit fragmentarily,
within the subject already. Above all, and if not by the means proposed, then by
others (not least through the systematic identification of various cultural
patterns in a spatial sense), it seems to the writer that historians should now be
seeking ways in which to discover local 'societies' at the very start of their
investigations and therefore *before* they relate such societies to the landscape, to
'community' or to 'class', or even to the broader historical trends or processes
within which these societies had to function and adapt.

   The framework proposed here is inevitably both schematic and over-
simplified; much that might have been said has had to be ignored for want of
space; much that one would have liked to have known is not yet known. There
must, however, be a place in any subject both for the generalized reappraisal of
its field and for constructive speculation which may then be tested, refined, even
radically altered, by others. The framework in question, furthermore, is at least
internally logical in that it seeks not to confuse real social entities with
administratively, economically, or geographically defined entities which are

subsequently 'characterized' as social entities. On the contrary, it aims deliberately to bring into their proper relationship the two concepts of 'community' and 'society', by recognizing that both these terms are similarly multifaceted in their meanings: each relates, however imprecisely, to a membership in process, to a structure, and to sets of ideas and images concerning both the particular nature of that structure and also forms of cultural identification with a social territory. In the space available, membership has been discussed only at the different spatial levels of, and in the contrasting temporal dimensions of, both mobility and situational longevity; the study of structure has had to be confined to that most fundamental of societal bonds, kinship; and culture has only been dealt with contextually. Even at this somewhat superficial level of discussion, however, these three matters merge when the fundamental distinction between 'community' and any wider societal entity is drawn. The lineage, not the family, is the basic unit of society and the transmitter of its structures and of its traditions. In contrasting temporal terms the family, not the lineage, must be regarded as the basic unit of 'community'. Only at the community core do lineage and 'community' meet. It is no accident that historians have often failed to find dense kinship networks within certain communities; since everything points to the wider locality as the spatial 'unit' through which individuals or families circulated while taking their kinship links with them. It is that simple fact which allows us to sketch in, albeit in preliminary fashion, the possibility that there may be orders of social relations wider than the community awaiting identification if we would only start to look for them. The analytical stance adopted here then is quite opposite to that of those who work outwards from a single rural community to its 'social area'. Here, it is suggested, that in the countryside, we need to finds ways of identifying *groups* of linked communities before we work inwards in order to locate any one of these communities spatially in relation to its immediately environing social system. (In present contexts, it is only in the vicinities of towns that the social area is likely to prove a fruitful concept.) Even before that stage, indeed, where the evidence to some extent allows, we might be advised to look more widely still: to the level of the shire.

From these various considerations, it has been argued that the orders of social relations which are most relevant to English local historians are those that fit informally, in an upwardly logical sequence, into the interstices of our current and, largely formalized, objects of study. Community cores may relate most closely to fairly restricted dynastic neighbourhoods; many of those less rooted families – the 'temporary' visitors – within communities, and not a part of their cores, may relate mainly to the wider social environment of the *pays* or its subdivisions; yet others may relate to the over-arching society of the shire (which in spatial terms will never be exactly coterminous with the formal limits of the county as an administrative unit) and its component towns.

At this juncture we can return but briefly to a wider problem that has received only passing allusion in this discussion. Wherever we end the local historical quest for connection between provincial society and the national society, there will always be a provincial horizon – a cut-off point beyond which the concerns of the local historian begin to fuse with those of the national historian. For obvious reasons, the present discussion has had to concentrate on spatial orders of social relations no higher than that of the shire. The writer is convinced, however, that more attention should be paid by local historians to a higher but more intangible order still: an order that may be epitomized by the great provincial urban centre, like York or Exeter, which, in its significance as a 'capital', may embody some such culturally defined perception as 'the North' or 'the Western parts'.[2] Much is now known about such cities and the longer-distance migrational patterns of which they were the *foci*; a good deal less, however, has been written in an integrated way about the wider provincial contexts of which these centres are taken to be the expression, and from which most of those migrants came.

This series of spatially definable orders – from community core, to 'community' itself (whether rural or urban); to 'neighbourhood'; to the yet wider social and cultural locality that, away from the towns, may yet prove in its extent broadly to reflect a *pays* or its subdivisions; to the society of the shire; until we reach the level of the 'province' – represents no more than a rough and ready conceptual hierarchy, about which it may be useful for local historians to think. It is certainly not intended to imply that all these socio-spatial levels would have been equally bounded. Indeed, with certain suggestive exceptions to which attention has been drawn, especially at the shire level and also where the limits of certain *pays* are well defined, the purpose of this 'model' is to leave room for degrees of integration, both in spatial and in social terms. Not only are county boundaries commonly overlapped by tracts of homogeneous countrysides or cut across by major routes of communication, but clearly social links between the different socio-spatial orders concerned were forged in numerous other ways: by the geographical widening of marriage horizons at superior social levels (and hence of kinship connections), by seasonal labour patterns, by the activities of the wayfaring community, and by that longer-distance migratory process that may have concerned as much as ± 20 per cent of those living in the pre-industrialized world, to name but a few such factors.

The hierarchy in question, nevertheless, is a hierarchy of 'belonging' in Finberg's sense of that term, and as such remains entirely faithful to his original definition of English local history as an academic discipline. Where the present purpose differs from that earlier perception is in seeking not to separate local histories from the national history, but deliberately to find ways of linking the local to the national through a broadly identifiable sequence of overlapping and ever-widening micro-structures that might eventually be seen to coalesce with the macro-structure of the national society. By macro-structure is meant the formal and informal conventions that are held to apply nationally to such matters as family and kinship, the distribution of power and the social ordering of 'classes', expectations of local 'community' at various levels, and the perception of national allegiance and identity, all of which norms – and others – may be differently interpreted at geographically separated provincial levels. To such primary matters, indeed, even the institutionalized mechanisms of government – important though these are – must always remain secondary when we are creating a social base-map. One has only to recall the helpless manner in which the over-centralized governments of today seek unsuccessfully to net local societies in the broad meshes of newly defined local government boundaries, only to find that yet again many people have swum safely through them, to realize the inadequacy of most administrative units as objects for societal analysis. It is the degree of misfit between the untidiness of society on the ground and the ideal tidiness of administrative units that is of significance at this level. To test that lack of 'fit', then, it must be stressed again, we first must identify our local 'societies'. In terms of the underlying relationship between the macro-structure and the micro-structures on the ground, indeed, much more important than administrative institutions will be the manner in which 'national' power is informally distributed and supra-regional influence is filtered down to the level of 'neighbourhoods'. If, consequently these last could be spatially defined, the situation and distribution of noble and gentry estates within and amongst them might tell us much about the ways in which the tentacles of patronage and clientage at different periods reached down to local dynastic grass-roots.

To insist on the preliminary need to identify local societal areas, however, is certainly not to claim that such 'societies' remained for ever static, or even always 'survived' in some sense from earlier times: as Professor Alan Everitt has emphasized, human regions tended eventually to supersede older, physical ones.[3] Continuities there undoubtedly were, but just as it proved necessary for the pioneers of the subject to define chronological frameworks for the material origins, growth and decline of types of community, so too may it prove necessary to do the same in the rather different and more slippery contexts of local societies and their contrasting forms of cultural self-identification. For the early development of such societies, for example, will not necessarily synchronize with the first stages in the life-cycles of each of the individual communities of which they are composed. Such synchronicities may chime at periods of 'primary' settlement (but even here, problems of continuity from yet earlier periods need to be recalled) or during the later colonization – within relatively short spans of time – of virgin woodland or moorland, for instance; but opportunities of this kind will be rare indeed. Societal developments do not commonly occur on the uninhabited surface of a *tabula rasa*. On the contrary, societal genesis or, outside the towns, gradual metamorphosis is more likely to happen on the basis of groups of pre-existing settlements that slowly and almost imperceptibly change their characters under the new influences which they come to share in common: the expansion of population in hitherto sparsely settled areas, or the development of craft regions from the later Middle Ages onwards, and, as a common corollary to this, the developing pervasive influence of urban centres. In this sense, and as Alan Everitt has recently implied from a different vantage point from that argued here, it is proper to think of English society 'as an amalgam of different societies all at varying stages in their evolution, all influencing each other, yet all developing in their own way, moving forward at different periods and at different paces, so that one finds older societies co-existing often with equal vigour, alongside the new.'[4] To this we might add that such societies may also expand or contract in spatial terms according to the varying influences to which each is subject at different periods.

The problem of chronology is one that will have to be faced. If dynastic neighbourhoods in the countryside only emerged distinctively during or after the later seventeenth century,[5] then the narrowest socio-spatial level of analysis above that of the community which has been suggested here will need to be viewed perhaps in elastic terms. The later seventeenth century, like the age of 'deserted villages', was one of population contraction: in both cases, the last mentioned in particular when in some regions surviving villages were commonly interspersed with numerous atrophied communities,[6] the likely geographical range of kinship neighbourhoods may have shrunk. In periods of fast-rising population like the later sixteenth and earlier seventeenth centuries, by contrast, these neighbourhoods could well have gradually expanded over somewhat more extensive localities than it has been possible to indicate here: the relevant work has simply not been done for such periods.

The further back in time we move, the more difficult too is it to test the identities and the compositions of shire societies. With the exception of the surname evidence, the information to hand at present is late. But if the eighteenth century especially stands out as the temporal apotheosis of the county – the period *par excellence* of the county town, of county regiments, of nascent county cricket involving different levels of society, and of county clubs or societies in the metropolis[7] – the sense of county had been present long before and not simply in the medieval sense of a *communitas* to be represented by local gentry in the House of 'Communes'. Even in the sixteenth century, some local dialects were being associated with single counties, while earlier still, the intake of some Oxford and Cambridge halls and colleges was overtly biased towards scholars from particular shires. On the other hand, we know nothing as yet about the nature of those local 'societies' which inhabited, and may have been largely confined to smaller, sometimes already antique, territories: those under the immediate control of powerful franchise-holders – the possessors of medieval liberties like the Soke of Bury St Edmunds – which cut across any such discrete identity as the shire itself may have then possessed as a social unit. In the north and in the Welsh Marches in particular, this is a major problem which medievalists will eventually need to confront.

That said, the shire divisions of this country (and, indeed, sometimes their major subdivisions, as possibly in the cases of East and West Kent) are extraordinarily ancient: as positively identifiable administrative units, only a minority have been in existence for markedly less than a whole millennium. Many may have had yet longer histories still, even pre-histories.[8] As from the earliest documentable periods, shires frequently appear to reflect divisions of the people into broadly identifiable localized societies.[9] It is certainly not the present intention to revive the old arguments for racial causation that once used to be offered for a number of institutional and settlement features in English history; but where modern geneticists are drawing maps which seem to isolate, however crudely, certain identifiable hereditary factors in particular regions like Derbyshire,[10] we may have to accept that in the last resort the continuities inherent in the scientific laws of probability with respect to the gene pool are not lightly to be disregarded. To that extent at least, English local historians may need to temper their current preoccupations with those 'influences' (though sometimes they read like determinants) which are heavily topographical.

But if exciting new fields of investigation might thus be opened to the local historian, he above all can hardly be expected to relegate to a side-line that which ever has been the peculiar object of his pursuit: the reconstruction of local 'community'. 'Community', it may be urged, has to be understood in the contexts of the various social-spatial levels discussed and in both a long-term and a short-term temporal dimension. On the one hand, 'community' might be regarded as an expression of a wider social territory and its culture simply because every community represents a staging-post in the long-term process of ceaseless, inter-generational, circular mobility throughout the environing local-ity or shire in question. On the other hand, each community, being uniquely structured, will stand in a different kinship or cultural relationship to the local 'society' of which it is but a part. Whatever the case, the concept of 'community' is far too valuable to be taken to connote only the bounded society of a Pacific island, or some unrealistic abstraction which artificially divides all human activity within one settlement into different sets of data.[11] Modern anthropological investigations into contemporary English rural society show that 'communities' are well able to distinguish themselves. The indigenous inhabitants of such a rural community today, even when in a small inter-related minority, may, like their forefathers, also marry into, or be related to, families in other settlements in the neighbourhood; but simultaneously they demarcate their territory from that of their neighbours through their variously shared image of, and their identification with, the named place in which they live; and thus they signify their separate 'possession' of it.[12] (The same of course may be said of those many people who still staunchly claim loyalty to a named county.) A sense of belonging more or less simultaneously to a variety of societal levels does not diminish the significance of any one of them: every community may boast its own idiosyncratic annual calendar, for example, but elements of that calendar will also owe much to acknowledged rhythms in the outside world: to the shared seasonal rhythms of a farming region or those of commerce and industry, to the cycles of the church year, to the diary of local government, and to the tempo of the realm itself – not least to the births, marriages and deaths of monarchs and princes.

Given some relationship between 'community' and its environing social system, however, it might well prove productive to think about rather different forms of categorization from those in current use. First, it may be worth seeking ways in which to integrate both rural and urban 'societies' along the same spectrum. In other words, a town *plus its immediate vicinity*, which will vary in range according to both the town's status and its changing attractive powers, and from which it draws most heavily in terms of marriage partners, kinship connections, and its regular labour force, might be regarded as simply the most concentrated form of local 'society' (with its own component 'communities' – parochial or occupational – and its own dynastic neighbourhoods which are either connected to the surrounding countryside or even, if it is large enough, restricted to the town's own inhabited confines, including the suburbs). Such a 'nucleated' society, the leading characteristics of which will be fading towards its margins, might be contrasted to the more 'dispersed' form of society that may, to a greater or lesser extent, be associated with the villages, hamlets or isolated farmsteads within a traditionally conservative *pays*.

Secondly, within such 'societies', even within 'neighbourhoods', some communities – and not only small towns – may prove to be central to such systems while others will not be. In the former instance, certain communities might be regarded both as *foci* and as impulse-centres for the local activation and perpetuation not only of kinship relations but also of customary culture, whether that relates to work or to other attitudes. In extreme cases, not least at or near certain 'edges' of shire societies, and possibly also where native concentrations are strongest towards the 'centres'of shire societies, such traditionally 'strong' communities may themselves exist in linked groups, and then act in the first instance as a barrier towards a neighbouring shire, and in the second instance, as the cultural hub of the parent shire society. Other types of community by contrast might be more or less peripheral to such systems, and again in two ways. On the one hand, some communities, singly or even in groups, might be regarded as socially intermediate between two neighbouring 'societies' in the sense that their memberships are characterized by a rapid turnover of families who may be either attracted more or less equally in opposite directions simultaneously, or pulled towards one powerful rival society like an urban area or a craft region in particular. On the other hand, such traditionally 'weak' communities, in the sense that their memberships and their cultural attitudes will be but marginally tied to established local kinship networks and to local customary ways, may also include the communal precursors of some fresh societal re-arrangement in the district as a whole.

Speculative as such a form of categorization inevitably must be, it might be claimed nevertheless that it does represent an appropriate synthesis of the societal approach that has been proposed in this paper. This system of classification, so summarily outlined here, might allow us to adopt something more like a synoptic view of a regional 'society' as a whole because it is posited in terms that are relational: relational in the sense that, at the abstract level suggested, both 'town' and 'country' may be brought into some sort of logical comparative perspective; relational in that it applies to a hierarchy of ever-widening socio-spatial orders; relational in terms of social space; and relational within the frame of time since allowance is made not only for physical mobility, but also for both that which has been communally or societally 'accomplished' and that which is potential. It therefore allows for change.

Whether the application of such a scheme, or of one similarly posited, may prove possible, however, only time itself will tell. For present purposes it may simply serve as a reminder that, beyond and between the current rural and urban objects of the local historical pursuit, there surely lurk many other levels of regional societal reality that should be recoverable, and which no student of English past society, and certainly not the local historian, can afford to ignore. In seeking to uncover some of the historical secrets of our national society in contexts peculiar to the provinces, there may even be a place for a form of local history *per se* after all.

Notes

Foreword

1. H. P. R. Finberg, *The Local Historian and His Theme*, University College of Leicester, Department of English Local History Occasional Papers, 1 (1952).
2. Asa Briggs, 'The Leicester School', *New Statesman*, 15 Feb. 1958, 206–7.

Chapter 1. Local History and National History

1. G. H. Tupling, *The Economic History of Rossendale*, Publications of the University of Manchester Economic History Series, IV (1927).
2. J. D. Chambers, *Nottinghamshire in the Eighteenth Century. A Study of Life and Labour under the Squirearchy* (2nd edn, 1966), xxiii-xxiv.
3. W. G. Hoskins, *Industry, Trade and People in Exeter 1688–1800*, History of Exeter and the South-West Research Group Monograph VI (1935), 28.
4. W. G. Hoskins and H. P. R. Finberg, *Devonshire Studies* (1952), 10–11.
5. H. P. R. Finberg, 'The local historian and his theme', reprinted in H. P. R. Finberg and V. H. T. Skipp, *Local History: Objective and Pursuit* (1967), 9.
6. *Ibid.*, 12–13.
7. Finberg, 'Local history', in Finberg and Skipp, *op.cit.*, 39.
8. *Ibid.*, 32.
9. W. G. Hoskins, 'The writing of local history', *History Today*, 11 (1952), 487–91, and his *Local History in England* (1959), 11–14.
10. W. G. Hoskins, *English Local History: The Past and the Future*, An Inaugural Lecture (1966), 22.
11. M. W. Beresford, 'Herbert Finberg: an appreciation', in Joan Thirsk (ed.), *Land, Church and People: Essays Presented to Professor H. P. R. Finberg, Agricultural History Review*, 18, suppl. (1970), vii.
12. M. M. Postan, 'Glastonbury estates in the twelfth century', in his *Essays on Medieval Agriculture and General Problems of the Medieval Economy* (1973), 276 n.45. I owe this reference to the kindness of Dr H. S. A. Fox.
13. H. P. R. Finberg, *Roman and Saxon Withington: A Study in Continuity*, University College of Leicester, Department of English Local History Occasional Papers, 8 (1955), 40.
14. W. G. Hoskins, *The Midland Peasant. The Economic and Social History of a Leicestershire Village* (1957), xviii-xix.
15. W. G. Hoskins, *Essays in Leicestershire History* (1950), *passim*; *idem*, 'The Elizabethan merchants of Exeter', in S. T. Bindoff, J. Hurstfield,, C. H.

Williams (eds.), *Elizabethan Government and Society: Essays Presented to Sir John Neale* (1961), 163–87.

16. W. G. Hoskins, 'English provincial towns in the early sixteenth century', in his *Provincial England* (1963), 68–85.

17. H. P. R. Finberg, 'Charltons and Carltons', in his *Lucerna* (1964), 144–60.

18. H. P. R. Finberg, 'The boroughs of Devon', *Devon and Cornwall Notes and Queries*, 24 (1951), 203–9, and 27 (1956), 27–8; *idem*, 'The genesis of the Gloucestershire towns', in H. P. R. Finberg (ed.), *Gloucestershire Studies* (1957), 52–88; Maurice Beresford and H. P. R. Finberg, *English Medieval Boroughs: a Handlist* (1973).

19. Maurice Beresford, *New Towns of the Middle Ages: Town Plantation in England, Wales and Gascony* (1967).

20. W. G. Hoskins, 'The wealth of medieval Devon', in Hoskins and Finberg, *Devonshire Studies*, 215–18; 'English provincial towns'; *Local History in England*, 174–8.

21. Maurice Beresford, *The Lost Villages of England* (1954).

22. M. W. Beresford and J. K. S. St Joseph, *Medieval England: An Aerial Survey* (1958).

23. Hoskins, *Industry, Trade and People in Exeter*, 18–19. E.g. Peter Clark and Paul Slack, 'Introduction' to Clark and Slack (eds.), *Crisis and Order in English Towns 1500–1700. Essays in Urban History* (1972), 1–56; Peter Clark and Paul Slack, *English Towns in Transition 1500–1700* (1976), 1–81.

24. E.g. D. A. Iredale, 'Canal settlement: a study of the canal settlement at Barnton in Cheshire between 1775 and 1845' (Ph.D. thesis, University of Leicester, 1967); Alan Everitt, 'The lost towns of England', in his *Landscape and Community in England* (1985), 109–27; E. M. Carus-Wilson, 'Evidence of industrial growth on some fifteenth-century manors', in Carus-Wilson (ed.), *Essays in Economic History*, II (1962), 151–67; David Hey, *The Rural Metalworkers of the Sheffield Region*, University of Leicester, Department of English Local History Occasional Papers, 2nd ser., 5 (1972), 5–10; *idem*, 'Industrialized villages', in G. E. Mingay (ed.), *The Victorian Countryside* (1981), 1, 353–63; Raphael Samuel, 'Quarry roughs', in Samuel (ed.), *Village Life and Labour* (1975), 139–263; Alan Everitt, *The Pattern of Rural Dissent: The Nineteenth Century*, University of Leicester, Department of English Local History Occasional Papers, 2nd ser., 4 (1972), 32–40; Simon Pawley, 'Lincolnshire coastal villages and the sea, c.1300–c.1600: economy and society' (Ph.D. thesis, University of Leicester, 1984); Mary Prior, *Fisher Row: Fishermen, Bargemen and Canal Boatmen in Oxford, 1500–1900* (1982), 105–7, 129.

25. Joy MacAskill, 'The Chartist Land Plan', in Asa Briggs (ed.), *Chartist Studies* (1959), 325–30; Dennis Hardy, *Alternative Communities in Nineteenth-Century England* (1979).

26. Dennis Mills, 'English villages in the eighteenth and nineteenth centuries: a sociological approach', *Amateur Historian*, 6 (1963–5), 271–8. Cf. J.H. Martin, 'The parliamentary enclosure movement and rural society in Warwickshire', *Agricultural History Rev.*, 15 (1967), 19–39.

27. Mills, *op.cit.*, 78–9.

28. *Ibid.*, 64–97; J. Obelkevich, *Religion and Rural Society: South Lindsey, 1825–1875* (1976), 11–14; Everitt, *The Pattern of Rural Dissent*, 20–32; Samuel, *op.cit.*, 15–17; M. A. Havinden, *Estate Villages* (1966), *passim*.

29. W. G. Hoskins, 'Regional farming in England', *Agricultural History Rev.*, 2 (1954), 3–11; H. C. Darby, 'Some early ideas on the agricultural regions of England', *Agricultural History Rev.*, 1–5 (1953–7), 30–47.

30. Joan Thirsk, *Fenland Farming in the Sixteenth Century*, University College of Leicester, Department of English Local History Occasional Papers, 3 (1953); *idem, English Peasant Farming: the Agrarian History of Lincolnshire from Tudor to*

Recent Times (1957); *idem*, 'The farming regions of England', in Thirsk (ed.), *The Agrarian History of England and Wales*, IV, *1500–1640* (1967), 1–112.

31.   Eric Kerridge, 'Agriculture, c.1500–c.1793', *V.C.H. Wiltshire*, IV (1959), 43–64; *idem, The Agricultural Revolution* (1967), 41–180.

32.   Joan Thirsk, 'Industries in the countryside', in F. J. Fisher (ed.), *Essays in the Economic and Social History of Tudor and Stuart England in Honour of R. H. Tawney* (1961), 70–88.

33.   Alan Everitt, 'Farm labourers', in Thirsk (ed.), *The Agrarian History of England and Wales*, IV, 396–465; *idem, The Pattern of Rural Dissent, passim; idem*, 'River and wold: reflections on the historical origin of regions and *pays*', *J. Historical Geography*, 3.1 (1977), 1–19 (repr. in his *Landscape and Community in England* (1985), 41–59).

34.   Alan Everitt, 'Country, county and town: patterns of regional evolution in England', *Trans. Royal Historical Soc.*, 5th ser., 29 (1979), 84–5.

35.   Everitt, *The Pattern of Rural Dissent*, 44–5; *idem*, 'River and wold', 14–17; *idem*, 'The making of the agrarian landscape of Kent', in his *Landscape and Community*, 82–90; *Continuity and Colonization: the Evolution of Kentish Settlement*, Communities, Contexts and Cultures: Leicester Studies in English Local History, ed. Charles Phythian-Adams (1986), *passim*.

36.   In addition to the authorities cited in nn. 32 and 33, see e.g., Joan Thirsk, 'Horn and thorn in Staffordshire', *North Staffordshire J. of Field Studies*, 9 (1968), 1–16; David Hey, *The Rural Metalworkers of the Sheffield Region*; J. M. Martin, 'Village traders and the emergence of a proletariat in south Warwickshire, 1750–1851', *Agricultural History Rev.*, 32 (1984), 179–88; David Hey, 'The pattern of nonconformity in South Yorkshire 1660–1851', *Northern History*, 8 (1973), 86–118; R. W. Malcolmson, *Life and Labour in England* (1981), 111–12.

37.   David Underdown, *Revel, Riot and Rebellion: Popular Politics and Culture in England 1603–1660* (1985), *passim*.

38.   Everitt, 'River and wold', 19.

39.   *Ibid.*

40.   Everitt, *Continuity and Colonization, passim*.

41.   Thirsk, 'The farming regions', 1.

42.   Hoskins, *The Midland Peasant*; Cicely Howell, *Land, Family and Inheritance in Transition: Kibworth Harcourt 1280–1700* (1983); Philip A. J. Pettit, *The Royal Forests of Northamptonshire*, Publications of the Northamptonshire Record Society, XXIII (1968), 141–82; David G. Hey, *An English Rural Community: Myddle under the Tudors and Stuarts* (1974); J. R. Ravensdale, *Liable to Floods: Village Landscape on the Edge of the Fens, A.D. 450–1850* (1974); Margaret Spufford, *Contrasting Communities: English Villagers in the Sixteenth and Seventeenth Centuries* (1974).

43.   Spufford, *op.cit.*

44.   Victor Skipp, *Crisis and Development: An Ecological Case Study of the Forest of Arden 1570–1674* (1978).

45.   J. D. Marshall, 'The study of local and regional "communities": some problems and possibilities', *Northern History*, 17 (1981), 203–30; *idem*, 'Why study regions? (1)', *J. of Regional and Local Studies*, 5.1 (1985), 15–27; 'Why study regions? (2): Some historical considerations', *ibid.*, 6 (1986), 1–12.

46.   W. G. Hoskins, *Devon*, A New Survey of England, ed. Jack Simmons (1954); C. M. L. Bouch and G. P. Jones, *The Lake Counties 1500–1830: A Social and Economic History* (1961); C. W. Chalklin, *Seventeenth-Century Kent: A Social and Economic History* (1965).

47.   A. L. Rowse, *Tudor Cornwall: Portrait of a Society* (1941).

48.   A. G. Dickens, *Lollards and Protestants in the Diocese of York 1509–1558* (1959); R. B. Smith, *Land and Politics in the England of Henry VIII: The West Riding of*

Yorkshire 1530–1546 (1970); Mervyn James, *Family, Lineage and Civil Society: A Study of Society, Politics, and Mentality in the Durham Region 1500–1640* (1974).

49. J. S. Morrill, *Cheshire, 1630–1660: County Government and Society during the English Revolution* (1974); Anthony Fletcher, *A County Community in Peace and War: Sussex, 1600–1660* (1975); A. Hassell Smith, *County and Court: Government and Politics in Norfolk 1558–1603* (1974); Peter Clark, *English Provincial Society from the Reformation to the Revolution: Religion, Politics and Society in Kent 1500–1640* (1977); and e.g. M. J. Bennett, 'A county community: social cohesion amongst the Cheshire gentry, 1400–1425', *Northern History*, 8 (1973), 24–44.

50. E.g. Clive Holmes, 'The county community in Stuart historiography', *J. of British Studies*, 19.2 (1980), 54–73.

51. Clark, *English Provincial Society*, 3.

52. But see *ibid.*, and Underdown, *op.cit.*

53. Lawrence Stone and Jeanne C. Fawtier Stone, *An Open Elite? England 1540–1880* (1984), 43–7; A. M. Everitt, *The Local Community and the Great Rebellion*, The Historical Association (1969), 18–22; A. M. Everitt, *Transformation and Tradition: Aspects of the Victorian Countryside*, The Second Helen Sutermeister Memorial Lecture, University of East Anglia (1982), 12–23, 32–3.

54. From an extensive literature see especially Everitt, 'Country, county and town', 88–106; Peter Borsay, 'The English urban renaissance: the development of provincial urban culture, c.1680–1760', *Social History*, 5 (1977), 581–603; Peter Clark, 'The migrant in Kentish towns 1580–1640', in Clark and Slack (eds.), *Crisis and Order in English Towns 1500–1700*, 117–63.

55. E.g. J. C. Holt, *The Northerners: A Study in the Reign of King John* (1961); William E. Kapelle, *The Norman Conquest of the North: The Region and its Transformation, 1000–1135* (1979). The outstanding exception to this assertion is Mervyn James: see his *Society, Politics and Culture: Studies in Early Modern England* (1986).

Chapter 2. Local History: The Need for a Framework

1. E.g. Margaret Spufford, *Contrasting Communities: English Villagers in the Sixteenth and Seventeenth Centuries* (1974); David G. Hey, *An English Rural Community: Myddle under the Tudors and Stuarts* (1974); Mary Prior, *Fisher Row: Fishermen, Bargemen and Canal Boatmen in Oxford, 1500–1900* (1982); Keith Wrightson and David Levine, *Poverty and Piety in an English Village* (1979); D. M. Palliser, *Tudor York* (1979); C. V. Phythian-Adams, *Desolation of a City: Coventry and the Urban Crisis of the Later Middle Ages* (1979).

2. Edward Britton, *The Community of the Vill: A Study in the History of the Family and Village Life in Fourteenth-Century England* (Toronto, 1977); Wrightson and Levine, *op.cit.*; Dr Alan Macfarlane's demonstration of the anthropological approach to the analysis of Earls Colne and Kirby Lonsdale is eagerly awaited. In the meantime, see his admonitory general discussion of the problem (which curiously ignores a range of local historical findings): Alan Macfarlane in collaboration with Sarah Harrison and Charles Jardine, *Reconstructing Historical Communities* (1977).

3. H. P. R. Finberg, 'Local history', in Finberg and V.H.T. Skipp, *Local History: Objective and Pursuit* (1967), 32.

4. *Ibid.*, 33, 5–6, 34–5.

5. See n.1 *supra*.

Chapter 3. National Society and Local Societies: The Quest for Connection

1. Fernand Braudel, *L'Identité de la France* (Paris, 1986) – only two out of four

projected volumes being completed.

2. B.A. Holderness, ' "Open" and "close" parishes in the eighteenth and nineteenth centuries', *Agricultural History Rev.*, 20 (1972), 132.

3. W. M. Williams, *A West Country Village: Ashworthy* (1963), 38–43, 109.

4. Margaret Spufford, *Contrasting Communities: English Villagers in the Sixteenth and Seventeenth Centuries* (1974), 57.

5. Keith Wrightson and David Levine, *Poverty and Piety in an English Village* (1979), 78.

6. J. D. Goodacre, 'Lutterworth in the sixteenth and seventeenth centuries: a market town and its area' (Ph.D. thesis, University of Leicester, 1978); David Fleming, 'A local market system: Melton Mowbray and the Wreake Valley 1549–1720' (Ph.D. thesis, University of Leicester, 1981).

7. Alan Everitt, 'Country, county and town: patterns of regional evolution in England', *Trans. Royal Historical Soc.*, 5th ser., 29 (1979), 90–1, 93–4.

8. Alan Everitt, 'Country-carriers in the nineteenth century', *Journal of Transport History*, n.s. 3.3 (1976), 191.

9. Alan Everitt, *Landscape and Community in England* (1985), 112–13.

10. David G. Hey, *An English Rural Community: Myddle Under the Tudors and Stuarts* (1974), 218, 8, 223–4. See also the various reservations on the relationship between geography and society that are expressed in Spufford, *op.cit.*, *passim*.

11. E.g. M. A. Watkinson, 'Population change and agrarian development: the parishes of Bradley, Scartho, and Humberston c.1520–c.1730' (M.Phil. thesis, University of Leicester, 1984), *passim*.

Chapter 4. A Possible Societal Framework

1. *Census of Great Britain, 1851: Population Tables*, II, i (HMSO, 1854), civ.

2. E. A. Wrigley and R. S. Schofield, *The Population History of England 1541–1871: A Reconstruction* (1981), 529.

3. The table is based on *1841 Census of Great Britain . . . Population III* (1971), modern pagination, 84; and *Census of England and Wales for the year 1861, III, General Report* (HMSO, 1863), 162. The influence of Poor Law Settlements on residential patterns is difficult to assess.

4. For the ranking of the county in 1841 (when its native density amounted to 83.7 per cent of the population) see p.29 *supra*. I am extremely grateful to Mr Peter Gray (Bedford College of Higher Education) for generously putting at my disposal both his unpublished calculations and a detailed distribution map based on the 1841 census (which does not appear in his thesis, 'The pauper problem in Bedfordshire from 1795 to 1834' (M.Phil. thesis, University of Leicester, 1975), and of which figure 1 is a generalized version. For the long-term demographic background of the county, see the pioneering piece by Lydia M. Marshall, *The Rural Population of Bedfordshire, 1671–1921*, Publications of the Bedfordshire Historical Record Soc., XVI (1934). A broadly similar pattern to that shown on figure 1 has now been identified by Mr Geoffrey Brown for the north-eastern sections of the Leicestershire boundary. Very broadly, the parishes in the vicinity with the lowest native densities lie more or less on either side of that boundary not only in Leicestershire but also in the adjacent parts of Nottinghamshire, Lincolnshire and Rutland.

5. B. A. Holderness, 'Personal mobility in some rural parishes of Yorkshire, 1777–1822', *Yorkshire Archaeological J.*, 42 (1967–70), 445.

6. Peter Clark, 'Migration in England during the late seventeenth and early eighteenth centuries', *Past and Present, 83* (1979), 65, 67. Cf. J. Cornwall, 'Evidence of population mobility in the seventeenth century', *Bull. of the Institute of Historical Research*, 40 (1967), 150, 146.

7. Dorothy McLaren, 'The Marriage Act of 1653', *Population Studies*, *28* (1974), 325–6. I owe this reference to the kindness of Dr Susan Wright.
8. Richard McKinley, *The Surnames of Lancashire*, English Surnames Series, IV, ed. Richard McKinley (1981), 441.
9. *Ibid.*, 77–153, 385–421; George Redmonds, *Yorkshire West Riding*, English Surnames Series, I, ed. Richard McKinley (1973), 91–259.
10. W. G. Hoskins, 'A history of the Humberstone family', *Trans. of the Leicestershire Archaeological Soc.*, *20* (1937–9), 241 (and map)–287.
11. W. G. Hoskins, *Leicestershire Yeoman Families and their Pedigrees* (1974), repr. with minor amendments from *Trans. of the Leicestershire Archaeological Soc.*, *23* (1946), 24.
12. Cicely Howell, *Land, Family and Inheritance in Transition: Kibworth Harcourt 1280–1700* (1983) 45, 60, 210, 216; 50.
13. Alan Everitt, *Landscape and Community in England* (1985), 312.
14. J. M. Martin, 'The parliamentary enclosure movement and rural society in Warwickshire', *Agricultural History Rev.*, *15* (1967), 28–9. Cf. Margaret Spufford, *Contrasting Communities: English Villagers in the Sixteenth and Seventeenth Centuries* (1974), 86–7, 108–9.
15. Alan Everitt, *Transformation and Tradition: Aspects of the Victorian Countryside* (1982), 7–11.
16. David Hey, *An English Rural Community: Myddle under the Tudors and Stuarts* (1974), 11, 200. Cf. Holderness, *op.cit.*, 446.
17. Mary Prior, *Fisher Row: Fishermen, Bargemen and Canal Boatmen in Oxford, 1500–1900* (1982), *passim*; Everitt, *Transformation and Tradition*, 27. Cf. Holderness, *op.cit.*, 448. Craftsmen, agricultural labourers and stockingers all loom large in the kinship reconstruction of Claybrooke parish, Leicestershire, which is discussed p. 41 *infra*.
18. Everitt, *Landscape and Community*, 317–19, 322–4.
19. W. G. Hoskins, *Essays in Leicestershire History* (1950), 132; Peter Laslett, *Family Life and Illicit Love in Earlier Generations* (1977), 79.
20. Howell, *op.cit.*, 241–3, 248–9; Clark, *op.cit.*, 73, 81–83.
21. R. S. Schofield, 'Age specific mobility in an eighteenth century rural English parish', *Annales de Démographie Historique* (1970), 264, 270–1; Ann Kussmaul, *Servants in Husbandry in Early Modern England*, Interdisciplinary Perspectives in Modern History, ed. Robert Fogel and Stephan Thernstrom (1981), ch. 4; *idem*, 'The ambiguous mobility of farm servants', *Economic History Rev.*, 2nd ser., *34* (1981), 222–35.
22. F. G. Davenport, *The Economic Development of a Norfolk Manor 1086–1565* (1906), 96–7. Cf. C. C. Dyer, *Lords and Peasants in a Changing Society: The Estates of the Bishopric of Worcester 680–1540* (1980), 366; R. K. Field, 'Migration in the later Middle Ages: the case of the Hampton Lovett villeins', *Midland History, 8* (1983), 42.
23. See nn.29 and 31 *infra*. F. M. Stenton, 'The thriving of the Anglo-Saxon ceorl', in Doris Mary Stenton (ed.), *Preparatory to Anglo-Saxon England* (1970), 386; Reginald Lennard, *Rural England 1086–1135: A Study of Social and Agrarian Conditions* (1959), 20–1.
24. Clark, *op.cit.*, 59.
25. Keith Snell, 'Parish registers and the study of labour mobility', *Local Population Studies, 33* (1984), 29–43; A. J. Pain and M. T. Smith, 'Do marriage horizons accurately measure migration?', *ibid.*, 44–8.
26. Jeremy Millard, 'A new approach to the study of marriage horizons', in Michael Drake (ed.), *Population Studies from Parish Registers* (1982), 143; E. Sunderland, 'Comment on "History and blood groups in the British Isles" by W. T. Potts', in P. H. Sawyer (ed.), *Medieval Settlement* (1976), 255; C.F. Küchemann, A. J. Boyce and G. A. Harrison, 'A demographic and genetic

study of a group of Oxfordshire villages', in Michael Drake (ed.), *Applied Historical Studies* (1973), 212–13 – for the Otmoor 'countryside'.

27. John R. Cole, 'Marriage horizons in East Kent, 1620–1640', John Nichols Prize-Winning Essay, University of Leicester (1977), 52–8.

28. Mary Dobson, ' "Marsh fever" – the Geography of malaria in England', *J. Historical Geography, 6* (1980), 374–5 and n.

29. A. Constant, 'The geographical background of inter-village movements in Northamptonshire and Huntingdonshire 1745–1943', *Geography, 33* (1948), 83–5; P. J. Perry, 'Working-class isolation and mobility in rural Dorset, 1837–1936', *Trans. Institute of British Geographers, 46* (1969), 131, 138.

30. Constant, *op.cit.*, 85 n.5. Cf. McLaren, *op.cit.*, 325–6; while the same obstruction by a river has also been uncovered by my pupil, Mrs Anne Mitson (to whom I am most grateful for this information), with regard to the Trent so far as the marriage-horizons of certain parishes in south-west Nottinghamshire were concerned in the seventeenth century. Cole, *op.cit.*, 59, 71–2.

31. Bessie Maltby, 'Easingwold marriage horizons', in Drake (ed.), *op.cit.*, 115, Moira Long and Bessie Maltby, 'Personal mobility in three West Riding parishes 1777–1812', *ibid.*, 126, 129, 131–2; Cole, *op.cit.*, 64; Prior, *op.cit.*, 105–6, 224.

32. Cole, *op.cit.*, 30, 64–70. Depositions in ecclesiastical courts seem somewhat unrepresentative of female migratory experiences when set against urban sex ratios: David Souden, 'Migrants and the population structure of later seventeenth-century provincial cities and market towns', in Peter Clark (ed.), *The Transformation of English Provincial Towns* (1984), 137, 149–61.

33. I am most grateful to Mrs Mary Carter for information from her researches on St Ives for this point, and similarly to Mrs Anne Mitson for contributing details of her Nottinghamshire material.

34. Although located in the county of Cumberland, for present purposes Alston should be counted as outside it since the parish lay ecclesiastically in the diocese of Durham, and physically on the eastern side of the watershed.

35. F. M. Stenton, 'Pre-Conquest Westmorland', in D. M. Stenton (ed.), *op.cit.*, 214–23.

36. B. J. Buckatzsch, 'The constancy of local population and migration in England before 1800', *Population Studies, 5* (1951–2), 62–7. For broad patterns of relative permanence, judged largely by the surname evidence, in the topographical circumstances of the Lake Counties generally, see J. D. Marshall, *Old Lakeland* (1971), 11–31, 49–51, 53, 106–16.

37. I am most grateful to Mr Alan Storm for kindly making this information available to me. See also A. Storm, 'Robin Hood's Bay: a character study of a coastal community with special reference to the period 1780–1880 and the shipping boom (M.A. dissertation, University of Leicester, Department of English Local History, 1978).

38. J. A. Tuck, 'Northumbrian society in the fourteenth century', *Northern History, 6* (1971), 22–39; R. T. Spence, 'The pacification of the Cumberland borders, 1593–1628', *Northern History, 13* (1977), 59–160.

39. Sunderland, *op.cit.*, 261.

40. Morgan I. Watkin, 'A B O blood groups, human history and language in Herefordshire with special reference to the low B frequency in Europe', *Heredity* (1965), 83–95.

41. Charles Phythian-Adams, 'Rutland reconsidered', in Ann Dornier (ed.), *Mercian Studies* (1977), 78–9 and map. The outlines of the possible evolution of Claybrooke parish are discussed in Phythian-Adams, *Continuity, Fields and Fission: The Making of a Midland Parish*, University of Leicester, Department of English Local History Occasional Papers, 3rd ser., 4 (1978), especially 33–5.

42. Charles Phythian-Adams, 'Leicester and the emergence of its county' in Phythian-Adams (ed.), *The Norman Conquest of Leicestershire and Rutland: A Regional Introduction to Domesday Book* (1986), 9–11.

43. John Prest, *The Industrial Revolution in Coventry* (1960), 2, fig. 1; W. Felkin, *An Account of the Machine Wrought Hosiery Trade* (1845), 7, repr. in *The Framework Knitters and Handloom Weavers* (New York, 1972).

44. Martyn F. Wakelin, *English Dialects: An Introduction* (1972), 10, 91, 104, 107, 121, 124.

45. Alan Roberts, 'The farming inhabitants of Appleby and Austrey: two midland parishes, 1550–1700' (Ph.D. thesis, University of Adelaide, 1984), *passim*, and esp. 204–5; Keith Wrightson and David Levine, *Poverty and Piety in an English Village* (1979), 85.

46. E.g. Hey, *op.cit.*, 59; Wrightson and Levine, *op.cit.*, 79. An appropriate rider to these comments is to be found in *Leicester Mercury*, 14 Aug. 1986, 13, in a report about the proposed transferral of Appleby Magna (and three other Leicestershire villages) to Warwickshire: 'Villagers have made it clear in countless letters . . . and at public meetings that they will have to be "dragged" across the Leicestershire-Warwickshire boundary, and even if they lose the fight Leicestershire will always be home.' The chairman of Appleby parish council spoke of Atherstone (Warks.) as follows: 'We have no affinity with the place . . . we feel that for Ashby and Coalville and the actual city of Leicester. Those are the places we go to shop, those are the places we have transport to, and Leicestershire is where we want to remain. We can't stand the thought of being in Warwickshire.'

47. J. D. Goodacre, 'Lutterworth in the sixteenth and seventeenth centuries: a market town and its area' (Ph.D. thesis, University of Leicester, 1981), *passim*.

48. *Ex inf.* Dr David Hey.

49. William White, *History, Gazetteer, and Directory of Leicestershire* (1846), 384–86.

50. Public Record Office, HO 107/597/15, 16, 17, 18, 19, HO 107/1136/16. All the following interim results represent the outcome of a long-term adult education group project which included a family reconstitution using not only the parish register, but also evidence from the headstones in Claybrooke Parva churchyard, from Anglican registers in adjacent parishes and from a dissenting congregation's register from Ullesthorpe. Those involved have included Mr R. J. Abbot, Mrs F. Aitkenhead, Mrs J. E. Bourn, Mrs K. H. Bray, the late Rev. R. Cowling, Mrs A. Gough, Dr J. D. Goodacre, Mrs J. Kerr, Mr and Mrs D. Price, Mr and Mrs V. Robinson, Mrs W. Warren and Mr C. Yewlett.

51. Bittesby, Wigston Parva and Smockington respectively, although the last-named strictly speaking lay outside the parish.

52. Of 100 brides and grooms who came from places outside Claybrooke parish but from within the ten-mile radius, 68 per cent came from the east of Watling Street.

53. *Census of Great Britain, 1851, Population Tables*, II, ii, 599.

54. 6 partners from Hinckley; 12 from Lutterworth.

55. But excluding Bittesby and Smockington (see n. 51 *supra*) because of insufficient linkages.

56. The numbers of households *per* settlement in 1841 were as follows: Wigston Parva, 9; Claybrooke Parva, 16; Wibtoft, 23; Ullesthorpe, 129; Claybrooke Magna, 93 plus 2 at High Cross.

57. Wrightson and Levine, *op.cit.*, 87, table 4.5. The general pattern was therefore much more similar to modern Gosforth: W. M. Williams, *The Sociology of an English Village: Gosforth* (1956), 72. Preliminary results from Claybrooke, based on 95 households, suggest that 84 per cent of the

relationships traced between households were between parents and children or between siblings.

58. Claybrooke Magna, Claybrooke Parva (the pivot of the system with 37.5 per cent of its 16 households looking both to Claybrooke Magna and to Ullesthorpe), Ullesthorpe and Wibtoft.

59. To judge from the distribution of local farming family names in White, *op.cit.*, Claybrooke Magna and Parva, and Ullesthorpe connected with adjacent villages to the east and south-east (Ashby Parva and Bitteswell), but not to the north (Frolesworth); whereas Wigston Parva's nominal links were, with the exceptions of Ashby Parva and Frolesworth, with places to the north-west of the Fosse Way.

Chapter 5. Conclusion: Some Implications

1. E. Sunderland, 'Comment on "History and blood groups in the British Isles" by W. T. Potts', in P. Sawyer (ed.), *Medieval Settlement* (1976), fig. 24.2. For the wider potential of the surname evidence, see G. W. Lasker, *Surnames and Genetic Structure*, Cambridge Studies in Biological Anthropology (1985).

2. E.g. D. M. Palliser, 'York under the Tudors: the trading life of the northern capital', in Alan Everitt (ed.), *Perspectives in English Urban History* (1973), 39–59; *idem, Tudor York* (1979) *passim*. For the most sensitive discussion of the 'provincial' dimension, see J. Le Patourel, 'Is Northern history a subject?', *Northern History, 12* (1976), 1–15. For an attempt to discount the distinctiveness of the north at this period, however, see B. W. Beckinsale, 'The characteristics of the Tudor North', *Northern History, 4* (1969), 67–83.

3. Alan Everitt, 'Country, county and town: patterns of regional evolution in England', *Trans. Royal Historical Soc.*, 5th ser., 29 (1979), 107.

4. Alan Everitt, *Landscape and Commnity in England* (1985), 6.

5. *Ibid.*, 313–17.

6. Maurice Beresford and John G. Hurst (eds.), *Deserted Medieval Villages: Studies* (1971), 27–9.

7. At least in the debates of the Williamsburg conference mentioned in Acknowledgments *supra*. I am particularly grateful to Professor Peter Clark for this point about London societies.

8. P. H. Sawyer, *From Roman Britain to Norman England* (1978), 62–3.

9. In other cases, of course, some counties, like Warwickshire, represent the outcome of later artificial territorial re-arrangements.

10. Sunderland, *op.cit.*, 256.

11. Alan Macfarlane in collaboration with Sarah Harrison and Charles Jardine, *Reconstructing Historical Communities* (1977), 4–20.

12. E.g. Marilyn Stathern, *Kinship at the Core* (1981); Clement Harris, *Hennage: A Social System in Miniature* (New York, 1974); A. P. Cohen (ed.), *Belonging: Identity and Social Organisation in British Rural Cultures* (1982).